WRITING SCIENTIFIC PAPERS IN ENGLISH SUCCESSFULLY

YOUR COMPLETE ROADMAP

Ethel Schuster,
Haim Levkowitz,
Osvaldo N. Oliveira Jr.
(Editors)

WRITING SCIENTIFIC PAPERS IN ENGLISH SUCCESSFULLY

YOUR COMPLETE ROADMAP

Andover, Massachusetts, USA
and
São Carlos, Brazil
2014

Editors
Ethel Schuster
Haim Levkowitz
Osvaldo N. Oliveira Jr.

Authors
Sandra M. Aluísio
Carmen Dayrell
Valéria D. Feltrim
Haim Levkowitz
Osvaldo N. Oliveira Jr.
Ethel Schuster
Stella E. O. Tagnin
Valtencir Zucolotto

Copyediting
Merav Levkowitz

Design and Cover
Rodrigo Rosalis
Rosalis Designer
www.rosalis.com.br

Library of the São Carlos Institute of Physics, University of São Paulo

Writing scientific papers in English successfully: your complete roadmap /
   edited by Ethel Schuster, Haim Levkowitz and Osvaldo N. Oliveira Jr. –
   São Carlos: 2014.
   192p.

   ISBN 978-85-88533-97-4

   1. Technical writing. I. Schuster, Ethel, ed. II. Levkowitz, Haim, ed.
III. Oliveira Jr., Osvaldo N., ed.

                                                808.0665 – dc22

PREFACE

WRITING SCIENTIFIC PAPERS IN ENGLISH SUCCESSFULLY: YOUR COMPLETE ROADMAP

Osvaldo N. Oliveira Jr.,
Ethel Schuster,
and Haim Levkowitz

MOTIVATION: THE IMPORTANCE OF SCIENTIFIC WRITING

Scientific writing has been recognized as a key ingredient in science and technology because of the need to share ideas and findings. Distinguished scientists have stated that the writing of a paper may account for "half the importance" of any scientific work. Indeed, successfully publishing papers is the primary indicator of a scientist's performance. Yet students rarely receive any training in scientific writing. Their only way to learn what the main components of a paper are and how papers are organized is by intuition, which may be ineffective and/or inefficient, or by trial and error, which may waste a lot of their time and hurt their confidence. Consequently, scientists at various levels in their careers often end up writing papers with poor grammar and structure and that lack clear focus. Many such papers do not get published despite their valuable contributions.

WRITING IN ENGLISH: ITS IMPORTANCE AND CHALLENGES

Having to communicate in English is necessary in today's world. English is now the *lingua franca* not only of science, but also of the speedy communications we depend on, namely the

Internet, the World Wide Web, social media, crowdsourcing, and other information-sharing resources.

The challenge of producing well-written papers is especially hard for non-native speakers of English, who account for the majority of scientists around the world. Effective scientific writing requires both mastery of the English language and proficiency in the specific academic genre.

Many years of teaching courses in scientific writing have taught us that the combination of the language barrier and the lack of knowledge of the academic writing style can have a detrimental effect on the quality of writing produced by non-natives in English. In many cases, students are unable to identify their main difficulties and whether these are the result of the lack of English proficiency or of their poor organization of ideas. Students seldom realize that it is harder to produce (that is, write) in a foreign language than to consume (that is, read and understand).

We have developed a strategy to tackle the problems faced by writers who are new to the scientific writing genre and style. This strategy can help both non-natives attempting to overcome the language barrier and native speakers of English. The strategy consists of using a variety of techniques and tools. Using this strategy will help students grasp the skills necessary for language-independent scientific writing. The strategy, its techniques, and its tools are at the heart of this book. We provide a complete roadmap for you, our reader, to learn the skills necessary to write well and successfully.

OVERVIEW OF THE BOOK

This book is divided into two parts: the first part provides the theoretical foundations of scientific writing. The second part details the strategies, techniques, and tools that are at the heart of our approach.

Chapter 1 lays out the specific characteristics of scientific writing and how it differs from other writing styles. Chapter 2 is devoted to the models that define scientific writing, introducing concepts that are central to the understanding of this writing style. You cannot write a good paper without reading good papers. In Chapter 3, we offer you an efficient and effective technique for reading many papers (and other publications). This should help you not only with your writing skills, but also with your general research tasks. Chapter 3 will also teach you how to read and annotate documents to build your own collection of well-written text samples. This collection is referred to as a corpus. Chapter 4 introduces the notion of corpus linguistics, which is a linguistics-based approach that uses text collections to help you determine the most appropriate language patterns for your own writing. Chapter 5 walks you through a set of computer-based tools that can guide you through the writing process and help you verify that your writing achieves your goals as best as possible. Finally, Chapter 6 teaches you how to systematically identify textual patterns that are prevalent in each section of a scientific paper. Learning to use these patterns well will aid you in writing papers using the language and style accepted by your research community.

ACKNOWLEDGMENTS

This book is the result of many years of teaching, research, and development involving contributions by countless colleagues and students. Special thanks are due to the researchers and students of the Interinstitutional Center for Computational Linguistics (NILC), Brazil, for their research and development of software writing tools. We are especially thankful to Professors Adalberto Pessoa Jr. and Ana Campa of the Faculty of Pharmaceutical Sciences at the University of São Paulo, Brazil, for their contributions to SciPo-Farmácia. The authors are also grateful to the São Carlos Institute of Physics and to the Institute of Mathematics and Computer Science, both at the University of São Paulo, for their support in the form of research on writing tools and graduate courses in scientific writing. Financial support has been crucial over the years, and we are thankful for grants from CNPq, CAPES, and FAPESP in Brazil. We also thank the University of São Paulo for providing a grant for Ethel Schuster and the Fulbright Foundation for a grant for Haim Levkowitz to support both as visiting professors at the University of São Paulo. Finally, we wish to thank Merav Levkowitz for her skillful copyediting and manuscript management.

About the Authors

Sandra Maria Aluisio is a lecturer in computer science at the São Carlos Institute of Mathematics and Computer Science at the University of São Paulo, Brazil, and a member of the Interinstitutional Center for Research and Development in Computational Linguistics (NILC). Her main interests are natural language processing and artificial intelligence in education, primarily using machine learning.

Carmen Dayrell currently works as a senior research associate at the ERSC Centre for Corpus Approaches to Social Science at Lancaster University in the United Kingdom. Her main research interests are corpus linguistics, discourse analysis, English academic writing, translation, and foreign language teaching.

Valéria Delisandra Feltrim is a lecturer in computer science in the Informatics Department at the State University of Maringá, Brazil, and a member of the Interinstitutional Center for Research and Development in Computational Linguistics (NILC). Her main interests are natural language processing and artificial intelligence in education.

Haim Levkowitz is a 42-year computing technologies veteran. He has been a computer science faculty member at the University of Massachusetts Lowell since 1989. He is a two-time recipient of a Fulbright award. His research interests are focused on human-information interaction.

Osvaldo N. Oliveira Jr. is a professor at the São Carlos Institute of Physics at the University of São Paulo, Brazil, and one of the founders of NILC. His main research interests are nanotechnology and natural language processing.

ETHEL SCHUSTER is a professor in the Department of Computer and Information Sciences at Northern Essex Community College. Her research interests focus on computational linguistics and computer science education. Throughout her career she has worked to encourage students, in particular women and minorities, to study computer science.

STELLA E. O. TAGNIN is a professor in English language, translation, and corpus linguistics in the Department of Modern Languages at the University of São Paulo. Her main interests are corpus linguistics applied to English learning and teaching, translation, and terminology.

VALTENCIR ZUCOLOTTO is a professor at the São Carlos Institute of Physics at the University of São Paulo, Brazil. His research focuses primarily on studies of nanomedicine and nanotoxicology and on the development of courses in scientific writing.

CONTENTS

1 THE FUNDAMENTALS OF SCIENTIFIC WRITING 17
Osvaldo N. Oliveira Jr., Ethel Schuster,
Haim Levkowitz, and Valtencir Zucolotto

    1.1 The need to write:
            the importance of publishing 19
          1.1.1 Getting the message across:
                    describing your research 20

    1.2 Steps to begin the writing process 22
          1.2.1 Organizing your ideas and results 22
          1.2.2 Organizing your paper 23
          1.2.3 Characteristics of scientific writing 24
          1.2.4 The typical structure of
                    a scientific paper 27

    1.3 In summary 28

2 MODELS FOR SCIENTIFIC WRITING 29
Sandra M. Aluísio, Osvaldo N. Oliveira Jr., and Valtencir Zucolotto

    2.1 Understanding the structure of
            scientific papers: rhetorical analysis 31

    2.2 Typical sections in a scientific paper:
            their content and depth 32
          2.2.1 Characteristics of scientific writing 32
          2.2.2 Title 33
          2.2.3 Abstract 33
          2.2.4 Introduction 35
          2.2.5 Methods and Materials 35
          2.2.6 Results 36
          2.2.7 Conclusion 37
          2.2.8 References 37
          2.2.9 Authors' guidelines 37

    2.3 The language style of a scientific paper 38

2.4 Models to explain the underlying
     structure of scientific papers:
     the introduction section 40
     2.4.1 The Swales Model 41
     2.4.2 The CARS (Creating a
            Research Space) model. 42
     2.4.3 Applying moves and steps
            to an abstract 48
     2.4.4 The Weissberg and Buker Model 50
     2.4.5 Aluisio and Oliveira's model 51

2.5 In summary 56

3 Reading, Annotating, Compiling,
and Producing Text for Scientific Papers 57
Osvaldo N. Oliveira Jr., Ethel Schuster, Sandra M. Aluísio and Haim Levkowitz

3.1 How to "skim" a scientific publication 59

3.2 "Learning-by-example": our strategy. 62
     3.2.1 What is annotation? 62
     3.2.2 Compiling your own corpus:
            manual annotation 63
     3.2.3 The Nine Steps 64

3.3 Automatic annotation 76
     3.3.1 Annotation guidelines 79
     3.3.2 A simple, fast, and reliable
            annotation procedure. 81

3.4 In summary 81

4 Using Corpus Linguistics to Overcome
the Language Barrier 83
Stella E.O. Tagnin

4.1 What is conventionality in language? 85

4.2 Colligations. 86

4.3 Collocations 86
    4.3.1 Verbal collocations 87
    4.3.2 Nominal collocations 87
    4.3.3 Adjectival collocations 88
    4.3.4 Adverbial collocations 89

4.4 Binomials 90

4.5 Conventional expressions 92

4.6 Corpus Linguistics 95

4.7 Building and investigating a corpus 103

4.8 In summary 113

4.9 Suggestions for exercises 114

5 WRITING TOOLS 115
Sandra M. Aluísio and Valéria D. Feltrim

5.1 SciPo-Farmácia and Scien-Produção 118
    5.1.1 SciPo-Farmácia 118
    5.1.2 Scien-Produção 127

5.2 MAZEA-WEB 129

5.3 SWAN 137

5.4 In summary 149

6 INSTRUCTIONAL PRACTICES USING
CORPUS LINGUISTICS 151
Carmen Dayrell

6.1 Textual patterns 153
    6.1.1 Why are textual patterns
           of special interest? 154
    6.1.2 Do novice and expert writers
           use similar patterns? 155
    6.1.3 Identifying textual patterns 156

6.2 Abstracts 157
   6.2.1 Abstracts: Stating the
       purpose of the study 158
   6.2.2 Identifying patterns in your
       own corpus 160
   6.2.3 Abstracts: describing results 161
   6.2.4 Identifying patterns in
       abstracts in your own corpus 162

6.3 The Introduction section 163
   6.3.1 Introducing what is
       known about the topic 163
   6.3.2 Diversifying patterns 165
   6.3.3 Indicating gaps in the literature 165
   6.3.4 Identifying patterns in
       introductions in your own corpus 166
   6.3.5 Citing previous work 166
   6.3.6 Describing the structure
       of the paper 168
   6.3.7 Identifying patterns in
       methods sections 169
   6.3.8 Identifying patterns in
       results and discussion sections 173
   6.3.10 Identifying patterns
       in acknowledgments 177

6.4 What have we learned? 177

7 CONCLUSION 179
Osvaldo N. Oliveira Jr., Ethel Schuster and Haim Levkowitz

APPENDIX A 183

BIBLIOGRAPHY 189

CHAPTER 1

Osvaldo N. Oliveira Jr.
Ethel Schuster
Haim Levkowitz
Valtencir Zucolotto

The Fundamentals of Scientific Writing

IN THIS CHAPTER WE WILL LEARN:

1. The need to write: the importance of publishing

2. Getting the message across: describing your research
    (a) What is the main contribution of your work?
    (b) Why is it important?

3. Steps to begin the writing process
    (a) Organizing your ideas and results
    (b) Organizing your paper

4. Characteristics of scientific writing

5. The typical structure of a scientific paper

1.1 THE NEED TO WRITE: THE IMPORTANCE OF PUBLISHING

Writing is both an art and a science. Writing requires organization that enables the reader to follow the ideas throughout the text, from its beginning to its end.

A recipe to make a cake, for example, enables a reader to follow this process in a given order. First, it instructs him or her to prepare the list of ingredients and their measurements. Next, it specifies the procedure for mixing those ingredients, ending with the final steps, after which the cake is ready to be consumed. Most written documents should aim to achieve the same continuity as a recipe does to grab the readers' attention.

We scientists have the goal and responsibility to share our ideas, discoveries, and developments with the scientific community and the world at large. One way in which we can achieve this goal — perhaps the most common and effective way — is by writing about our ideas, discoveries, and findings and publishing them in all sorts of media, including newspapers, magazines, scientific journals, books, conference proceedings, posters, and blogs. No matter what we write about, we must do it in a systematic, organized, and interesting manner, presenting the content in a clear and elegant way. Writing well is a necessary requirement — though not the sole one — for successfully publishing our work. We can show our readers how our ideas began, just like a recipe, which lists the set of ingredients that then ends up as the warm cake coming out of the oven.

1.1.1 GETTING THE MESSAGE ACROSS: DESCRIBING YOUR RESEARCH

The ability to communicate about one's scientific research requires thorough understanding of the importance and the value of the work being carried out. Often, it is difficult for students to answer the following two simple, but crucial, questions in a clear and concise manner:

1. What are the contributions of your work?
2. Why are these contributions important?

A growing number of funding agencies and publishers have established two criteria that they consider essential in evaluating your writing and scientific output: 1. the work's intellectual merit (mostly within its own field), and 2. its broader impact (on the world in general). Question 1 above ("What are the contributions of your work?") asks you to identify the intellectual merit of your work. This usually refers to intellectual challenges within your field and how your work helps to address them. Question 2 ("Why are these contributions important?") should address your work's impact within your field, but also its broader impact on the outside world.

Sometimes, for example, during poster sessions at conferences, one can observe that students are baffled by these questions. In some cases, they admit that they have never thought about them or that they have never been asked such questions. A successful strategy is to encourage students to answer these questions at levels that address three different audiences: (i) experts in their own field, (ii) scientists who work in other, possibly related, areas, and (iii) laypeople. When writing for laypeople, we suggest that you respond with straightforward answers as if you were speaking to your own grandmother (provided she is not a scientist herself) or to children.

The ability to answer these two questions well is directly related to the ability to communicate your message to various audiences. Sometimes students believe that their paper serves primarily as a way to describe their results. We take a different view: a paper is used to introduce new ideas and concepts along with their development and findings. In other words, scientists must focus on publishing their original ideas and concepts, not just their results. Obviously, a paper will only be published if the ideas or concepts are supported by hard data (results!). Furthermore, the ultimate aim of most research work is to provide results. For instance, a research group is trying to find new materials that behave as electrical superconductors at high temperatures. This is a desirable goal because of the technological advances that it could generate. If the group succeeds, they must convey their results as their most significant contribution. This result, a high-temperature superconductor, should be the highlight of their paper. However, the result came about as a consequence of an initial idea: the search for new superconductive materials. Even if the group fails in this quest, there may still be a justification for publishing a paper: the value of the idea to develop new materials is not diminished solely because a particular approach has failed. The paper can contribute by demonstrating that, while the goal of the research is valid, this particular method or approach used was not. Other scientists in the field who may have considered the same approach will save time and effort because they will learn about its failure.

1.2 STEPS TO BEGIN THE WRITING PROCESS

1.2.1 ORGANIZING YOUR IDEAS AND RESULTS

Getting ready to write in order to publish your research requires that you organize your ideas. Remember, your ideas are the essence of your research. We suggest that you first develop an outline, listing the components of the paper. You can then include the main ideas within those components and follow a logical order demonstrating their development and justification. You can do so by writing down the main ideas. Then, list the subordinate ideas and connect them. Try to avoid repetition.

Once you are ready to write about your research, you must have results to report. You should be able to answer these questions about your results:

- What are your key findings?
- What is the importance of your key findings to the field?
- Are your findings complete? If not, what is missing?
- What is the supporting evidence?
- Do they provide a basis for publication?

One suggestion is to lay out all the ideas and results and shuffle them around until you achieve an effective and logical progression to explain your argument, starting with your ideas and connecting them to your results and conclusions.

It is important that you use the appropriate language for your audience. Since you are writing for experts in your field, you need to adjust your language to their level of knowledge and expectation. Your language should be clear and concise, even when describing very complex research concepts. You should also write everything in English from the very beginning. Yes. Everything. In English. From the beginning! Write your lab notes in English. The more you write your ideas and notes in English, the easier it will be to put your paper together. You should avoid writing in any other language besides English.

1.2.2 ORGANIZING YOUR PAPER

You should present the ideas in your paper in a logical order. Inexperienced authors may tend, instead, to organize their papers in chronological order. It is possible for these two orders to coincide, whereby the paper is ordered in a logical manner as a result of the chronological order in which the research was carried out.

Note that the ideas obtained from the results may not be the same as those that initially drove the research. While the original ideas may be mentioned as the starting motivation, the paper should focus on whichever ideas support and promote your research. The paper should highlight the relationships among any and all of the ideas that eventually lead to the successful results reported. You should identify the ideas and results that are original. Only clearly stated original ideas and results may be published.

Writing a paper in a logical order enables the author to focus on the contributions of the research. In Figure 1.1, we show typical steps required to carry out the research process. Initially, you should select a scientific problem to focus on. You should ask whether a solution has been found (or proposed) for this problem. If no solution has been identified, you can proceed with the initial problem. If a solution exists, your next question should be whether you can improve on that solution. This process begins with an initial idea, which may be redefined as the research proceeds. The results from the initial ideas will most likely generate new ideas.

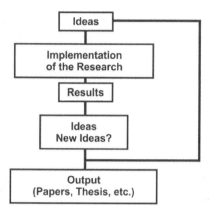

Figure 1.1: Flowchart illustrating the main processes in designing and implementing a research project, including the reporting of the main findings.

For example, if the only published or known solution to a computation problem is a slow algorithm, developing a faster algorithm would be considered a significant contribution. While planning your research, you should ask the following questions: "What are we contributing by solving this problem?" "Will we be able to publish the ideas or concepts demonstrated by the results?" "In which venue (a journal or a conference), could we publish this research?" Precise answers to these questions require well-founded, in-depth knowledge of your field. A survey of the literature showing what has been done and what is missing is necessary in order to advance said research field.

1.2.3 CHARACTERISTICS OF SCIENTIFIC WRITING

When scientists are ready to communicate their ideas and findings to the community at large, they do so by publishing papers in journals and conference proceedings in their field. These publications focus on specific areas of research and can serve as the nucleus for sharing the new findings with members of the same community.

Scientific writing tends to follow a systematic structure. Most scientific papers will follow a traditional format and may use specific language styles. Creativity should be demonstrated by the ideas and concepts — the content presented — not by creative writing. Most major publications are beginning to require that authors write within a given structure; sometimes the editors specify what each section should contain in their guidelines for authors. For instance, Nature, a world-renowned scientific magazine, provides authors with templates designed to organize their papers. This approach results in publications with a systematic and structured description of the research conducted.

Medicine & Science in Sports & Exercise
Issue: Volume 30(4), April 1998, pp 629-633
Copyright: © Williams & Wilkins 1998. All Rights Reserved.
Publication Type: [Special Communications: Methods]
ISSN: 0195-9131
Accession: 00005768-199804000-00023
Keywords: ACCELEROMETER, PHYSICAL ACTIVITY, EXERCISE, ENERGY EXPENDITURE

[Special Communications: Methods]

Validity of the computer science and applications (CSA) activity monitor in children

TROST, STEWART G.; WARD, DIANNE S.; MOOREHEAD, SUSAN M.; WATSON, PHILIP D.; RINER, WILLIAM; BURKE, JEANMARIE R.

Author Information
Department of Exercise Science, University of South Carolina, Columbia, SC; Department of Physiology, University of S John Morrison White Clinic, Center for Developmental Exercise and Nutrition Research. University of South Carolina, Lanca
Submitted for publication October 1996.
Accepted for publication September 1997.

ABSTRACT

Purpose: The purpose of this study was to evaluate the validity of the CSA activity monitor as a measure of children's physical activity using energy expenditure(EE) as a criterion measure.

Methods: Thirty subjects aged 10 to 14 performed three 5-min treadmill bouts at 3, 4, and 6 mph, respectively. While on the treadmill, subjects wore CSA (WAM 7164) activity monitors on the right and left hips. $\cdot VO_2$ was monitored continuously by an automated system. EE was determined by multiplying the average $\cdot VO_2$ by the caloric equivalent of the mean respiratory exchange ratio.

Results: Repeated measures ANOVA indicated that both CSA monitors were sensitive to changes in treadmill speed. Mean activity counts from each CSA unit were not significantly different and the intraclass reliability coefficient for the two CSA units across all speeds was 0.87. Activity counts from both CSA units were strongly correlated with EE ($r = 0.86$ and 0.87, $P < 0.001$). An EE prediction equation was developed from 20 randomly selected subjects and cross-validated on the remaining 10. The equation predicted mean EE within 0.01 kcal·min^{-1}. The correlation between actual and predicted values was 0.93 ($P < 0.01$) and the SEE was 0.93 kcal·min^{-1}.

Conclusion: These data indicate that the CSA monitor is a valid and reliable tool for quantifying treadmill walking and running in children.

Figure 1.2: Example of scientific paper from computer science.

Note these two examples, the first from computer science and the second from medicine. In the computer science example, shown in Fig. 1.2, the abstract is organized into four components: (i) purpose of the research; (ii) methods used to carry out the research; (iii) results obtained; and (iv) conclusions [1]. This structure supports sections of a typical organization and logical order identified in scientific writing. The medicine example (Fig. 1.3) has eight sections: (i) context, (ii) objective, (iii) design, (iv) setting, (v) participants, (vi) main outcome measures, (vii) results, and (viii) conclusions [2]. The first four sections support the background and purpose of the research study. The section on participants is required in studies that involve subjects or patients.

Individual sections may vary from one publication to another, but they will most likely include the four basic ones shown in the first example.

ORIGINAL ARTICLE

Brain Anatomy and Its Relationship to Behavior in Adults With Autism Spectrum Disorder

A Multicenter Magnetic Resonance Imaging Study

Christine Ecker, MSc, PhD; John Suckling, PhD; Sean C. Deoni, PhD; Michael V. Lombardo, PhD; Ed T. Bullmore, MB, FRCPsych; Simon Baron-Cohen, PhD, FBA; Marco Catani, MD, MRCPsych; Peter Jezzard, PhD; Anna Barnes, PhD; Anthony J. Bailey, MD, PhD; Steven C. Williams, BSc, PhD; Declan G. M. Murphy, MBBS, FRCPsych, MD; for the MRC AIMS Consortium

Context: There is consensus that autism spectrum disorder (ASD) is accompanied by differences in neuroanatomy. However, the neural substrates of ASD during adulthood, as well as how these relate to behavioral variation, remain poorly understood.

Objective: To identify brain regions and systems associated with ASD in a large, well-characterized sample of adults.

Design: Multicenter case-control design using quantitative magnetic resonance imaging.

Setting: Medical Research Council UK Autism Imaging Multicentre Study (MRC AIMS), with sites comprising the Institute of Psychiatry, Kings College London; the Autism Research Centre, University of Cambridge; and the Autism Research Group, University of Oxford.

Participants: Eighty-nine men with ASD and 89 male control participants who did not differ significantly in

Results: Adults with ASD did not differ significantly from the controls in overall brain volume, confirming the results of smaller studies of individuals in this age group without intellectual disability. However, voxelwise comparison between groups revealed that individuals with ASD had significantly increased gray matter volume in the anterior temporal and dorsolateral prefrontal regions and significant reductions in the occipital and medial parietal regions compared with controls. These regional differences in neuroanatomy were significantly correlated with the severity of specific autistic symptoms. The large-scale neuroanatomic networks maximally correlated with ASD identified by partial least-squares analysis included the regions identified by voxel-based analysis, as well as the cerebellum, basal ganglia, amygdala, inferior parietal lobe, cingulate cortex, and various medial, orbital, and lateral prefrontal regions. We also observed spatially distributed reductions in white matter volume in participants with ASD.

Figure 1.3: Example of scientific paper from medicine.

1.2.4 THE TYPICAL STRUCTURE OF A SCIENTIFIC PAPER

The format of a scientific paper usually includes the following components:

1. Title: a brief statement highlighting a proposed solution to a problem. The title is the author's first opportunity to "advertise" the paper and attract readers' attention; a poorly chosen title may cause a potential reader to choose to skip reading the paper altogether.

2. The authors' names, affiliations, and their contact information.

3. Abstract: a short summary of the paper. The abstract should "set the stage" by defining the problem the paper will discuss and summarizing the contributions of the paper toward solving that problem. It should also state any other contributions the paper claims to make to the field. The abstract is the second, and expanded, opportunity for the author to engage readers and make them want to continue reading.

4. Introduction: a brief description that sets the stage for the rest of the paper. The introduction should give a background description, a more detailed description of the problem, and its significance (its "**purpose**"), a critical survey of any previous solutions, and the "**gap**" — the actual new contribution this paper will offer to the field. Most introduction sections also provide an overview of the rest of the paper at the end of the section.

5. Methods and Materials: the research that was conducted to address the problem and how it was carried out. Here the authors should provide all the necessary details to make their research reproducible, that is, to make it possible for anyone with comparable background, preparation, and infrastructure to repeat or reproduce

the study or experiments. This is a common scientific way to verify (or <u>refute</u>) reported results.

6. Results and Discussion: Presentation of the data, interpretation, and discussion of the results.
7. Conclusions: What can one conclude from the findings?
8. References: Sources used during the research reported in the paper.

1.3 IN SUMMARY

In this chapter, we have learned that writing scientific papers follows a well-recognized style and structure. We further observed that the research process leading to a successful and published paper requires a set of steps that can be repeated and reproduced by anyone with comparable abilities.

In the following chapters, we will introduce approaches, techniques, and tools that will allow you to write a paper from beginning to end following this structure.

CHAPTER 2

Sandra M. Aluísio
Osvaldo N. Oliveira Jr.
Valtencir Zucolotto

Models for Scientific Writing

IN THIS CHAPTER WE WILL LEARN ABOUT:

1. The typical structure and sections of a scientific paper

2. Some models that have been proposed to characterize this organizational structure

As we saw in Chapter 1, scientific papers follow a well-known structure, with identifiable components (or sections). Let us go over these typical components before we examine them in detail, one by one: Abstract, Introduction, Methods and Materials, Results and Discussion, and Conclusions.

In the second part of this chapter, we provide a theoretical foundation for this structure by examining and discussing several models.

2.1 UNDERSTANDING THE STRUCTURE OF SCIENTIFIC PAPERS: RHETORICAL ANALYSIS

Before describing the models that explain the underlying structure of scientific papers, it is important to define rhetorical analysis and its role in shaping those models. Rhetorical analysis establishes the relationship between the content of an argument (or idea) and its form (how this idea is described or justified). Thus, the focus is to determine whether the argument gets the intended message across, that is, the form describes the content properly [3].

- What the argument is;
- what the focus of the argument is;
- what the take-away message the reader is expected to get is; and
- why this argument is important.

Once the content of the argument has been characterized, we must focus on its form or presentation, which is characterized by:

1. The language used to make the argument;
2. the type of text being used, e.g., compare, contrast, propose, or evaluate;
3. the evidence that is provided for the argument;
4. the expected audience; and
5. the specific terms and definitions that are introduced in the text.

2.2 TYPICAL SECTIONS IN A SCIENTIFIC PAPER: THEIR CONTENT AND DEPTH

In Figure 2.1 we illustrate, layer by layer, the typical structure of a scientific paper, its sections, and their content. The depth of the contents of each section may vary between general and specific, depending on the sections that make up the paper. Each section offers different information and has different goals and objectives. To accomplish these goals and objectives, we, as writers, need to use different language forms.

2.2.1 CHARACTERISTICS OF SCIENTIFIC WRITING

It is common for these sections to appear in the order described above, beginning with the introduction and ending with the conclusion. Note that this structure, while typical and common in papers within scientific fields that are inherently experimental, such as medicine, biology, chemistry, and experimental physics, is not universal. Papers in other disciplines, such as mathematics and computer science, may not, for example, include a Methods and Materials section.

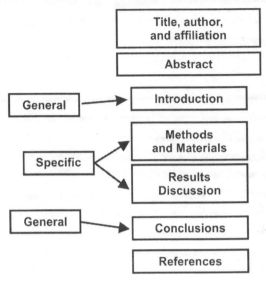

Figure 2.1: Typical structure of a scientific paper.

2.2.2 TITLE

A good title should attract the reader's attention. It should highlight the contents of the paper and provide the reader with مُقرّد a brief description of the research while remaining concise. It should be specific about the research and use key words that are associated with the outcome of the paper.

Following the title, the authors should be listed with their respective titles, institutions, and contact information.

2.2.3 ABSTRACT

The abstract plays a very important role within a paper. It is usually limited to 150 to 250 words, depending on the journal. An abstract can be written either in a descriptive or an informative
توصيفي   أ مزند

style. In a descriptive abstract, the authors describe what has been done, providing no descriptions or details of the results and the conclusions. A descriptive-styled abstract is suitable for a review paper, a summary of a book, or a book chapter, in which the authors may describe the contents of specific papers or books. This abstract type tends to discuss research ideas and results that may have been carried out by other researchers, not necessarily by the authors of the paper themselves.

The abstract of a scientific paper in which the authors report on their own research and its results should be written in the informative style. It should describe the major key concepts, findings, and results discussed in the paper. A reader should be able to grasp the researchers' main contributions from the abstract without having to read the entire paper.

The abstract should be structured as a micro version of the paper. It should highlight the research in an informative way, and it should be organized in a logical order. The Introduction section, a mini version of the paper, should be structured in the same logical order as the abstract, but should provide additional details. Note that abstracts of scientific papers include only text and no citations or references, unlike abstracts written for papers in other areas, such as the social sciences and the humanities. See Figure 2.2.

Although the abstract appears before the paper's complete content, it should provide a summary of the entire paper. We recommend that you write your abstract only after you have completed the paper.

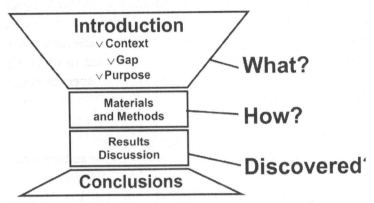

Figure 2.2: Typical structure of a scientific paper.

2.2.4 INTRODUCTION

The goal of the introduction is to provide the overall justification for the paper, beginning with a general discussion of the topic and introducing a specific research question. Just like the title and the abstract, the role of the introduction is to grab the reader's interest and to entice him or her to keep on reading. The introduction is a general, broad description of the research and its focus. See Figure 2.3.

2.2.5 METHODS AND MATERIALS

The Methods and Materials section describes the methods, materials, equipment, tools, supplies, and procedures that were used throughout the investigation. It may also include specific data analyses, examinations, and/or evaluations that will be used to describe the results. This section tends to be more specific due to the particular methods and materials described. Note that the Methods and Materials section is almost indispensable in sciences that are experimental in nature, such as medicine, biology, chemistry, and physics. It is crucial for the reproducibility of the research and its results. However, in sciences that are more theoretical than experimental, such as mathematics and some areas of computer science, it is rare to encounter a section entitled Methods and Materials. In such cases, the details of the research, which are important and necessary for reproducibility, are provided in another section or other sections of the paper.

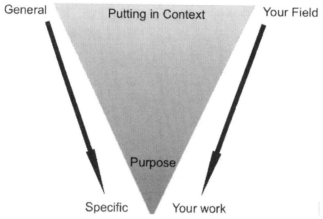

Figure 2.3: The introduction is a general, broad description of the research and its focus.

2.2.6 RESULTS

The Results and Discussion section describes the results identified in the research. It may include comments, discussions, and/or analysis of the findings. The results should be linked to the initial idea and the purpose or goal of the research so that the reader can observe the connection between the original idea and the results that were obtained.

2.2.7 CONCLUSION

The conclusion focuses on what was learned from the study. It may reiterate statements from key findings, interpretation of the research, and contributions to the field. It is common to mention any shortcomings of the current research and the limitations of the results. This may lead to a discussion of potential future work, especially for computer science-related areas. See Figure 2.4.

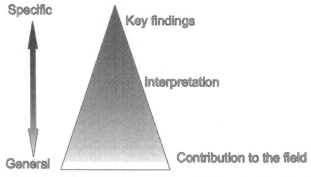

Figure 2.4: The conclusion extends specific key findings to broad contributions in the field.

2.2.8 REFERENCES

Any previous research that is related or relevant to the current research — including the author's own work — must be properly cited and referenced. The format and style of the references is almost always specified by the publication.

2.2.9 AUTHORS' GUIDELINES

Every publication, whether it is a journal or a conference proceeding, has its own set of authors' guidelines, which provides formatting specifications, such as page and margin dimensions, font types and sizes, figure and table formats, bibliography style, page limits, and submission procedures.

A paper that is perfectly written in all other aspects may be rejected even before the review process if it does not follow these guidelines to the letter. This is perhaps the most unfortunate reason for having your paper rejected, but, luckily, the easiest to avoid!

2.3 THE LANGUAGE STYLE OF A SCIENTIFIC PAPER

Each section or component of a scientific paper, in addition to being positioned in the paper in a specific order (as we saw above), may be written using a specific language style. Within each component or section, the writer may use a specific verb tense and a choice of voice (active versus passive). For example, to report on the results, one will, most likely, use the past tense: "We identified two different proteins."

Note the use of the active voice, as opposed to the passive voice. Many scientific journals have strict guidelines nowadays: they require authors to write primarily in the active voice in order to avoid convoluted passive voice forms. The instructions in the IEEE-Computer Author Guidelines state: "*Today's readers need to grasp information quickly. Extremely long articles presented in a passive writing style don't meet this need. Authors should strive for active verbs and straightforward declarative sentences, making every effort to help readers understand the concepts presented. An article should be comprehensible to all Computer readers, regardless of their specialty or research focus. Please note that accepted manuscripts will be edited, often extensively, to convey the magazine's unique voice and to conform to our style.*" [4].

Using the passive voice makes sentences longer and often harder to understand. And, passive voice phrases make it difficult to distinguish the original work by the authors from work accomplished by other researchers. Let us compare the two. Here is a passive voice example: "Mutants were obtained and used ..." **Who** obtained the mutants? **Who** carried out this experiment? In this case, due to the usage of the passive voice, the subject of the sentence (the "actor") is not identified and, thus, is distanced from the action being carried out. On the other hand, in the active voice version — "We obtained and used mutants..." — it is clear who carried out the work. You, the author, are expected to take responsibility for your work by writing in the active voice throughout the paper. Note that while you will encounter many papers that have been written in the passive voice, the tendency has been shifting, and publications increasingly expect active-voice writing. Also, note that while the writing style of some languages, such as Portuguese, tends to prefer the passive to the active voice, you will be writing your paper in English, to the specifications of the publication to which you intend to submit it. Therefore, you should not let the preferred style of your native language interfere with your scientific writing in English.

In Table 2.1, we list five linguistic features and their frequencies in four sections of a typical scientific paper, as identified by Swales [5]. We can see that the present tense of the verbs is preferred in the introduction and discussion sections, while the past tense is predominant in the methods and results sections. In general, papers will have a larger number of references in the introduction and discussion, the sections that typically describe the background and discuss literature review and related research. Understanding these features and their frequencies should help you write these sections with proper form and style.

	Introduction	Methods	Results	Discussion
Present tense	High	Low	Low	High
Past tense	Medium	High	High	Medium
Passive voice	Low	High	Varying	Varying
References	High	Low	Varying	High
Comments	High	Low	Varying	High

Table 2.1: Five linguistic features and their frequency in each of the four sections/components of a scientific paper, respectively. From ref. [5].

2.4 MODELS TO EXPLAIN THE UNDERLYING STRUCTURE OF SCIENTIFIC PAPERS: THE INTRODUCTION SECTION

The form and function of scientific papers are uniform throughout the world. The entire scientific community has accepted a standard structure for scientific papers in order to convey research ideas and results to their peers [5, p. 65]. With very few exceptions, English has become the language of scientific discourse. In order to successfully write and publish papers in English, you, the writer, must understand the concept of academic papers genre and how to apply this concept in order to properly structure your paper.

In the next section, we discuss three models that identify the different sections of a scientific paper. We focus on the Introduction section because it plays a strategic role: it provides the first in-depth impression of the paper. Thus, it must appeal to the reader so that he or she continues reading.

2.4.1 THE SWALES MODEL

John M. Swales [5, 6, 7] developed the concept of rhetorical moves to describe sections, or components, of scientific papers. He identified particular segments in papers in order to teach non-native speakers of English how to read and write papers. He introduced the notion of "moves" that make up specific sections within a paper.

"*The idea of clearly describing and explaining the rhetorical structure of a particular genre and of identifying each associated purpose is a contribution that can assist beginners and novices who do not belong to a specific discourse community. The move analysis of a genre aims to determine the communicative purposes of a text by categorizing diverse text units according to the particular communicative purpose of each unit. Each one of the moves where a text is segmented constitutes a section, revealing a specific communicative function, but this is linked to and contributes to the general communicative objective of the whole genre.*" [8].

Our approach follows Swales's definition of genre in academic texts. IIn his book Genre Analysis: English in Academic and Research Settings, Swales [5] uses the terms "communicative purpose" and "discourse community" to define genre, mainly because purpose, with its characteristic form and content, drives the conventions of each genre: "*A genre comprises a class of communicative events, the members of which share the same communicative purposes. Such purposes are recognized by the expert members of the discourse community of origin and, therefore, constitute the set of reasons (rationale) for the genus. These reasons shape the schematic structure of the discourse and influence and impose limits on the choice of content and style*" [5, p. 58].

Purpose plays an important role in characterizing genre. It guides us to treat genre as a set of linguistic rules without forgetting its social and cultural dimensions. Scientific writing is, in many ways, connected to the scientific method. The Oxford

English Dictionary [9] defines the scientific method as: "*a method of procedure that has characterized natural science since the 17th century, consisting in systematic observation, measurement, and experiment, and the formulation, testing, and modification of hypotheses.*"

2.4.2 THE CARS (CREATING A RESEARCH SPACE) MODEL

Swales proposed the "Creating A Research Space" (CARS) model, outlined in the Example 1 below. It uses rhetorical analysis, an approach that enables an author to justify his or her argument within a specific form. Swales's method is based on the analysis of academic and professional texts. It identifies typical rhetorical moves used in the introduction section of scientific papers in English. These moves can also describe the structure of a typical abstract, which itself summarizes the content (and sections) described in the Introduction.

Introduction

Move 1 Establishing a territory
Step 1 Claiming centrality and/or
Step 2 Making topic generalization(s) and/or Step 3 Reviewing items of previous research
Move 2 Establishing a niche
Step 1A Counter-claiming or Step 1B Indicating a gap or Step 1C Question-raising or Step 1D Continuing a tradition
Move 3 Occupying the niche
Step 1A Outlining purposes or
Step 1B Announcing present research
Step 2 Announcing principal findings
Step 3 Indicating Research Article structure

Example 1: Swales's Model of Rhetorical Moves in Research Articles (CARS)

The CARS model introduces a rhetorical structure with two hierarchical levels of information units: "moves" and "steps." A "rhetorical move" is defined as "a unit that performs a coherent communicative function in a spoken or written discourse" [7, p. 228]. These moves need to appeal to the reader as well as to justify the content of the section in the text. For instance, "Establishing a territory" is a move used to argue about the specific research in the text, which is common in the introduction. Within this move, the author can discuss related literature or justify the importance of the research using rhetorical steps that characterize how the argument can be written.

Each step serves a purpose. For example, Step 1 in Move 1, "Claiming centrality," appeals to the discourse community to accept the research reported in the paper as part of a major and well-established research area. Swales claims that these steps and moves can be written as a portion of a single sentence or in one or more sentences. Swales identified specific lexical items to indicate these moves and steps. Words such as "however," "no studies," "these studies indicate," and "this study attempts to" indicate whether a specific step or move is introduced. A sentence that starts with "However" may indicate a gap or a missing link. "No studies" can lead to an assertion that this study may be the first one to address the issue. "These studies indicate" points toward future work or missing parts in previous studies. And "this study attempts to" may be a way of showing how the current study aims at filling in some gap.

As an example, let us identify the steps and moves defined by Swales's model in the introduction section of a paper. We have chosen Pitler's paper [10] for this demonstration. The complete introduction is given in Example 2; its analysis, based on the CARS model, follows immediately after (Example 3).

Prepositions and conjunctions are two large remaining bottlenecks in parsing. Across various existing parsers, these two categories have the lowest accuracies, and mistakes made on these have consequences for downstream applications. Machine translation is sensitive to parsing errors involving prepositions and conjunctions, because in some languages different attachment decisions in the parse of the source language sentence produce different translations. Preposition attachment mistakes are particularly bad when translating into Japanese (Schwartz et al., 2003), which uses a different postposition for different attachments; conjunction mistakes can cause word ordering mistakes when translating into Chinese (Huang, 1983).

Prepositions and conjunctions are often assumed to depend on lexical dependencies for correct resolution (Jurafsky and Martin, 2008). However, lexical statistics based on the training set only are typically sparse and have only a small effect on overall parsing performance (Gildea, 2001). Unlabeled data can help ameliorate this sparsity problem. Backing off to cluster membership features (Koo et al., 2008) or by using association statistics from a larger corpus, such as the web (Bansal and Klein, 2011; Zhou et al., 2011), have both improved parsing.

Unlabeled data has been shown to improve the accuracy of conjunctions within complex noun phrases (Pitler et al., 2010; Bergsma et al., 2011). However, it has so far been less effective within full parsing — while first-order web-scale counts noticeably improved overall parsing in Bansal and Klein (2011), the accuracy on conjunctions actually decreased when the web-scale features were added (Table 4 in that paper).

In this paper we show that unlabeled data can help prepositions and conjunctions, provided that the dependency representation is compatible with how the parsing problem is decomposed for learning and inference. By incorporating unlabeled data into factorizations which capture the relevant dependencies for prepositions and conjunctions, we produce a parser for English which has an unlabeled attachment accuracy of 93.5%, over an 18% reduction in error over the best previously published parser (Bansal and Klein, 2011) on the current standard for dependency parsing. The best model for conjunctions attaches them with 90.8% accuracy (42.5% reduction in error over MSTParser), and the best model for prepositions with 87.4% accuracy (18.2% reduction in error over MSTParser).

We describe the dependency representations of prepositions and conjunctions in Section 2. We discuss the implications of these representations for how learning and inference for parsing are decomposed (Section 3) and how unlabeled data may be used (Section 4). We then present experiments exploring the connection between representation, factorization, and unlabeled data in Sections (5) and (6).

Example 2: Introduction of Pitler's paper [10].

Move 1: Establishing a territory

a: show that the general area is important, problematic, or relevant in some way (optional)

Prepositions and conjunctions are two large remaining bottlenecks in parsing. Across various existing parsers, these two categories have the lowest accuracies, and mistakes made on these have consequences for downstream applications. Machine translation is sensitive to parsing errors involving prepositions and conjunctions, because in some languages different attachment decisions in the parse of the source language sentence produce different translations.

Move 1: Establishing a territory

b. introduce and review items of previous research in the area (required)

The literature review can be organized:

1. Beginning with established major theories, then moving to theories associated with individual authors
2. In chronological order
3. According to the theories' topics or findings

Preposition attachment mistakes are particularly bad when translating into Japanese (Schwartz et al., 2003), which uses a different postposition for different attachments; conjunction mistakes can cause word ordering mistakes when translating into Chinese (Huang, 1983).

Prepositions and conjunctions are often assumed to depend on lexical dependencies for correct resolution (Jurafsky and Martin, 2008). However, lexical statistics based on the training set only are typically sparse and have only a small effect on overall parsing performance (Gildea, 2001). Unlabeled data can help ameliorate this sparsity problem. Backing off to cluster membership features (Koo et al., 2008) or by using association statistics from a larger corpus, such as the web (Bansal and Klein, 2011; Zhou et al., 2011), have both improved parsing. Unlabeled data has been shown to improve the accuracy of conjunctions within complex noun phrases (Pitler et al., 2010; Bergsma et al., 2011).

Move 2: Establishing a niche

a. Indicate a gap in the previous research, or extend previous knowledge in some way (required)

However, it has so far been less effective within full parsing — while first-order web-scale counts noticeably improved overall parsing in Bansal and Klein (2011), the accuracy on conjunctions actually decreased when the web-scale features were added (Table 4 in that paper).

Move 3: Occupying the niche

a. outline purposes or state the nature of present research (required)

b. announce principal findings

c. indicate the structure of the research paper

In this paper we show that unlabeled data can help prepositions and conjunctions, provided that the dependency representation is compatible with how the parsing problem is decomposed for learning and inference. By incorporating unlabeled data into factorizations which capture the relevant dependencies for prepositions and conjunctions, we produce a parser for English which has an unlabeled attachment accuracy of 93.5%, over an 18% reduction in error over the best previously published parser (Bansal and Klein, 2011) on the current standard for dependency parsing. The best model for conjunctions attaches them with 90.8% accuracy (42.5% reduction in error over MSTParser), and the best model for prepositions with 87.4% accuracy (18.2% reduction in error over MSTParser).

We describe the dependency representations of prepositions and conjunctions in Section 2. We discuss the implications of these representations for how learning and inference for parsing are decomposed (Section 3) and how unlabeled data may be used (Section 4). We then present experiments exploring the connection between representation, factorization, and unlabeled data in Sections (5) and (6).

Example 3: Instantiation of the CARS model on an Introduction section of a paper.

2.4.3 APPLYING MOVES AND STEPS TO AN ABSTRACT

In Example 4 below, we highlight steps and moves of the CARS model using an abstract ([11]) as an example:

Abstract

Move 1: Establishing a territory, Step 1: Claim centrality
In the early stages of neurodegenerative disorders, individuals may exhibit a decline in language abilities that is difficult to quantify with standardized tests. Careful analysis of connected speech can provide valuable information about a patient's language capacities.

Move 2: Establishing a niche, Step 2B: Indicating a gap
To date, this type of analysis has been limited by its time-consuming nature.

Move 3: Occupying the niche, Step 3B: Announcing present research
In this study, we present a method for evaluating and classifying connected speech in primary progressive aphasia using computational techniques. Syntactic and semantic features were automatically extracted from transcriptions of narrative speech for three groups: semantic dementia (SD), progressive nonfluent aphasia (PNFA), and healthy controls. Features that varied

significantly between the groups were used to train machine learning classifiers, which were then tested on held-out data.

Move 3: Occupying the niche, Step 3C Announce principal findings

We achieved accuracies well above baseline on the three binary classification tasks. An analysis of the influential features showed that in contrast with controls, both patient groups tended to use words which were higher in frequency (especially nouns for SD, and verbs for PNFA). The SD patients also tended to use words (especially nouns) that were higher in familiarity, and they produced fewer nouns, but more demonstratives and adverbs, than controls. The speech of the PNFA group tended to be slower and incorporate shorter words than controls. The patient groups were distinguished from each other by the SD patients' relatively increased use of words which are high in frequency and/or familiarity.

Example 4: Abstract of the paper [11].

There are lexical items in this abstract that enable us to identify steps and moves: "...has been limited by its time-consuming nature" **Move 2: Establishing a niche**; "In this study, we present a method for..." **Move 3: Occupying the niche, Step 1B: Announcing present research**; "We achieved accuracies..." **Move 3: Occupying the niche, Step 1B: Announcing principal findings**.

2.4.4 THE WEISSBERG AND BUKER MODEL

Weissberg and Buker [12] propose an alternative model for crafting the Introduction section of a paper. Their model consists of five initial stages. Each stage is then subdivided into steps, as shown in Example 5 below. The authors claim that the organization of a paper is basically the same regardless of its area and that their model works equally well for texts in the sciences, social sciences, and humanities.

- First Stage: Provides a context for the problem to be analyzed
  1. Facts related to the general area of research
  2. Identification of subareas
  3. Topic emphasis

- Second Stage: Checks aspects of the problem studied by other authors
  1. Quotes in which relevant information is prominently presented
  2. Reference to relevant research conducted by other authors
  3. Level of research activity in the area
  4. Quotes in which the author is prominent

- Third Stage: Emphasis of the need for more research
  1A. The reviewed literature is inadequate, or
  1B. Conflict/Problem not solved: a gap in the theory or practice, or
  1C. Issues not yet considered in the area, or
  1D. Topic extension/improvement

- Fourth Stage: The purpose or objective of the study

- 1A. Orientation of the article, or →present
- 1B. Orientation of the research →past.

- Fifth Stage: (Optional) Value/Justification of the study

Example 5: Model of the structure of Introduction sections

The authors emphasize specific linguistic features and/or patterns for each stage that can be successfully replicated by native and non-native English speakers.

In the fourth stage of this model, for instance, there is a specific verb tense used that is directly connected to that step. If the text refers to an article, letter, paper, or report, and the step described is "Orientation of the article," then the tense used is restricted to the present: "The aim of the present paper is to..." On the other hand, if the step is "Orientation of the research," referring to research as in a study, investigation, research, or experiment, then the past tense is used: "The purpose of this study was to..."

2.4.5 ALUISIO AND OLIVEIRA'S MODEL

Based on both Swales's and Weissberg and Buker's models, Aluisio and Oliveira developed a new, more specific model focusing on the introduction section of scientific papers [13]. Their model identifies (i) components, (ii) strategies, and (iii) messages. Components define the high-level category. Strategies provide the form by which to realize these components, and messages specify the language of the text.

Components, strategies, and messages in the introduction section

The Introduction section has eight components that can be realized linguistically through 30 strategies. A strategy can be made up of two or three rhetorical messages, from a set of 45 messages.

In Example 6 below we show the components and strategies that can make up the Introduction section of a scientific paper. Components are labeled with "C" followed by a number. Strategies are labeled with "S" and a number and are listed within each component. If a strategy is labeled with a letter after the number (as in S1A), it can be selected from all those labeled with "S1." Thus, using the strategy to "indicate main purpose" (S1), one can "present a novel approach, method, or technique" (S1B).

C1: Setting
S1 Introduce the research topic within the research area
S2 Familiarize terms, objects, or processes
S3 Argue about the topic's prominence

C2: Review
S1 Historical review
S2 Current trends
S3 General-to-specific ordering of citations
S4 Progress in the area
S5 Requirements for moving forward in the area
S6 State-of-the-art
S7 Compound reviews of the literature and their gaps
S8 Citations grouped by approaches

C3: Types of Gap
S1 Unresolved conflict or problem among previous studies
S2 Limitations of previous work
S3 Raise questions

C4: Purpose
S1 Indicate main purpose
S1A Solve conflict among authors
S1B Present a novel approach, method, or technique
S1C Present an improvement in a research topic
S1D Present an extension of author's prior work
S1E Propose an alternative approach
S1F Present comparative research work
S2 Specify the purpose
S3 Introduce additional purposes

C5: Methods and Materials
S1 List criteria or conditions
S2 Describe methods and materials
S3 Justify chosen methods and materials

C6: Main Results
S1 Present/emphasize results
S2 Comments about the results

C7: Value of the Research
S1 State importance of the research

C8: Layout of the article
S1A Outline the parts of the paper
S1B List issues addressed

Example 6: Main Components (C) and Strategies (S) that make up a typical introduction

Aluisio and Oliveira [13] developed their model after careful analysis of a corpus made up of 54 papers selected from two physics and materials science journals published between 1992 and 1994. About 80 percent of the introductions examined encompassed the following structure:

اما روش کردن

- Setting (C1)
- Review (C2)
- Type of Gap (C3)
- Purpose (C4)
- Main Results (C6)

Twenty four of the 54 introductions contained sublists of this structure. Nineteen samples included Value of Research (C7), Methods and Materials (C5), or Setting (C1) either in the same order as the one shown in the box above or in a different one by repeating components. For instance, they included a specific Review (C2) after Type of Gap (C3). The remaining 11 introductions had their own structure and style. Introductions that begin by stating the purpose (C4) highlight the authors' emphasis on a particular goal of their research: they want their readers to notice the importance of this goal. Only one introduction displayed a very complex structure, [C2, C4, C6, C5, C6, C2, C3, C6, C1], a characterization of a longer introduction.

Among the papers they examined, Aluisio and Oliveira found that the strategy "Argue about the topic's prominence" (S3) within the Setting component (C1) is often used to write the beginning of the Introduction section.

About messages

Aluisio and Oliveira identified 45 rhetorical messages in the Introduction section. These messages provide support to the identified strategies. Let us examine one example using a segment from an Introduction section. Within the Setting component (C1), we choose the strategy "Argue about the topic's prominence" (S3). This strategy can be instantiated with "*A great deal of interest has recently been stimulated by the use of organic materials in electroluminescent (EL) devices [1]*." The messages used here can be: (1) The claim is relevant; (2) the claim is currently valid; (3) The claim has been well established.

C1: Setting
    S3 Argue about the topic's prominence
        M2 Claim currently active

SETTING: ARGUING ABOUT THE TOPIC PROMINENCE

1) A great deal of interest has recently been stimulated by the use of organic materials in electroluminescent (EL) devices [1].

2) Organic molecules can be engineeered to possess specific functional properties, offering the possibility of obtaining intense fluorescence which can be tuned to a particular wavelength.

GAP: RESTRICTIONS IN PREVIOUS APPROACHES

3) However, the fabrication of EL devices with bright blue emission has proved difficult owing to the bathochromic shifts in emission wavelenfth which often occur betweeen solution and film spectra.

Figure 2.5: Part of one of the introductions

The Introduction examples in Figure 2.5 use the "Claim currently active" message in the "Argue about the topic's prominence" strategy. This is explained by the use of a time adverb "recently" which indicates that the research is currently active.

In Appendix A, we show the components and strategies identified and implemented for ALL sections of a scientific paper. They are used in the SciPo-Farmácia tool, a Web-based tool that was developed to support the writing of scientific papers. We discuss this tool in detail in Chapter 5.

Other sections, in particular those that are very specific to the research being reported, may have some variability depending on the field, topic, type of research or study, and more. For example, it is possible for a paper describing a biology, chemistry, or medical study to have a very different Methods and Materials section from that of a mathematics or computer science paper, which, as previously mentioned, may, in fact, not have a section with that title at all.

For the components and strategies for each section of a scientific paper, refer to Appendix A.

2.5 IN SUMMARY

In this chapter we have:

1. studied the typical structure of a scientific paper and its most common sections;
2. examined the models that have been used to study and analyze the scientific writing style;
3. identified the components of each section;
4. observed language patterns that serve best for each section component;

and

5. summarized the prevailing models that have been used to establish this analysis and characterization.

Chapter 3

Osvaldo N. Oliveira Jr.
Ethel Schuster
Sandra M. Aluísio
Haim Levkowitz

Reading, Annotating, Compiling, and Producing Text for Scientific Papers

IN THIS CHAPTER WE WILL INTRODUCE:

1. Strategies for effective reading large amounts of text

2. Strategies for building customized corpus

3. Ways to make automatic annotation in a corpus

3.1 HOW TO "SKIM" A SCIENTIFIC PUBLICATION

Every day, you, the scientist, are inundated with an ever-growing number of scientific and technical publications: journal and conference papers, books, Web sites, newsletters, and more. Many of these will be relevant to you; many will not. Linearly reading every word of each and every publication that comes your way is highly inefficient: you will end up reading many irrelevant pieces and will probably miss many relevant ones.

The strategy we present here should enable you to "separate the wheat from the chaff," and identify those publications that are of interest to you.

As we have seen in previous chapters, most scientific publications follow a typical structure. This structure can help us read through publications rapidly and efficiently. We suggest that you examine the contents of the paper in this order:

1. Title
2. Abstract
3. Conclusions
4. Introduction
5. Section headings, figures, captions
6. References

examine papers in this order.

We will describe each one of these in detail.

1. Read the **title** carefully. After reading the title, ask yourself: does this publication sound like it is of interest and/or relevance? If the answer is "NO," stop there. Otherwise, continue to the abstract.

2. Now turn to the **abstract**. A good abstract should tell you what this paper is all about, what problems it deals with, and what contributions it offers to the field. You should be able to have a pretty good idea of what a paper is all about from reading the abstract alone. Even better, many abstracts start with the background of the problem to be discussed, before proceeding to the paper's contributions. The first paragraph of this chapter serves as such an example. This paragraph sets the stage for introducing the focus of this chapter, which then appears in the second paragraph. If you skim over many abstracts, you will find that most abstracts only refer specifically to the paper itself about one-half to two-thirds of the way into the text. Search for the first sentence that starts with "In this paper ..." or "This paper ..." or "We show ..." and start reading there. Within two or three sentences, you will find out exactly what this paper's contribution claims to be.

3. Go all the way down to the **conclusions** section. Most conclusions offer a summary of the entire paper, emphasizing the paper's contributions and results. Often, the conclusions may outline what is missing and what could be done in the future. If you are interested in this problem, and are considering research along these lines, you might find opportunities here.

4. Examine the **introduction**. The introduction will most likely follow a similar pattern to that of the abstract, only a little longer and more detailed. Having already read the abstract and conclusion, you probably do not need

to read the introduction in its entirety, except perhaps the last part, where you will usually find the outline of the rest of the paper.

5. By now you should have a pretty good idea of whether you should continue reading or not. If you decide to continue, do not read any of the text for now. Go through the pages and just study the **section headers, figures and figure captions, and tables and their captions**. If the paper has any mathematical content and you are mathematically inclined, examine the mathematical expressions. سعد ربّي

6. Finally (for this round), take a look at the **bibliographic references**.

Look for references and authors that are familiar to you. If you find any, go back to the text and find where those are quoted. Often you will find an explanation about the differences between this paper and any previous work completed in this field. If you are familiar with the previous work, it will probably take you very little effort to understand what this paper is offering that is new and original.

For about eight or nine papers out of every ten, this is all you will need in order to understand the contents of this paper. By this point, you will have determined either that the paper does not merit any further reading, or that you already understand its contributions sufficiently. The remaining one or two papers will need to be re-read more thoroughly for more details. These may become your sources of reference.

Practice this with every scientific publication that lands on your desk. If it is a book, start with the Table of Contents, pick the chapters that sound most interesting, and repeat the same steps for each chapter. Read a journal the same way, first the table of contents and then the parts that are relevant to you.

If you follow this strategy, you will soon find out that you can cover a lot more material in less time than it has taken you in the past.

3.2 "LEARNING-BY-EXAMPLE": OUR STRATEGY

In this section we describe our "Learning-by-example" strategy, which has proven useful in scientific writing practice and in courses. It consists of guiding you, the student, to read papers and books in a systematic manner. Instead of concentrating on the content of the paper, we focus on how the paper is written and how its text conveys rhetorical messages (as defined in Chapter 2).

The strategy of "Learning-by-example" entails three goals, to:

1. carefully examine the written text in scientific papers,
2. annotate specific expressions that can be used as examples, and
3. compile and produce your own corpus.

3.2.1 WHAT IS ANNOTATION?

We define annotation (or "tagging") as the process of adding labels or notes (metadata) to documents while reading them. The annotation process entails two steps: (1) reading and deciding which fragment of the text to annotate, and (2) adding a label to that fragment, selected from a fixed, pre-defined set of tags. Annotation can be done **manually** by human annotators or **automatically** by a system trained to carry out this task.

Annotation can be done by highlighting, underlining, and/ or adding a label to the text.

After you collect and compile all the annotated fragments, you will have built your own corpus. This corpus will be made up of text that has been annotated with components and strategies as described in Chapter 2. The annotated text will help you, as a writer, to construct an argument, write a paper, and/or remember important facts.

In the excerpt below, taken from Figure 5 of Chapter 2, which refers to the CARS model, we see that the basic unit selected for annotation was a sentence:

> **Move 1: Establishing a territory, Step 1: Claim centrality**
> Metaphor is highly frequent in language, which makes its computational processing indispensable for real-world NLP applications addressing semantic tasks.

In this example, the moves and steps explain and justify the annotation of the sentence. This sentence serves to "establish a territory" by "claiming centrality" of the topic. (See Chapter 2 to refresh your memory about what these mean.)

3.2.2 COMPILING YOUR OWN CORPUS: MANUAL ANNOTATION

In the "learning-by-example" strategy, you will manually annotate papers that you need to read. We will guide you through this process, step by step.

The "learning-by-example" approach is outlined in a nine-step procedure, as follows. For each step, we will: (i) describe the step, (ii) explain how this step is implemented, and (iii) illustrate it with sample text from several papers, using text from those papers' abstracts to construct a new abstract. Our experience using and teaching this approach has shown us that compiling and using reference material is an effective way in which to learn the scientific discourse and its specific language. We emphasize the fact that this strategy should not be confused with plagiarism, in which complete text segments, concepts, and ideas, are copied verbatim and are then reused.

3.2.3 THE NINE STEPS

The procedure consists of nine steps, as follows:

Step 1 Select well-written texts from reliable sources that have been written by writers who possess the writing proficiency of a native speaker. Read the material critically, annotating expressions that convey important messages and that may be useful to imitate in the future.

    a.   Select scientific papers from reliable sources. Select papers published in your area of research. You should choose papers from journals with "high impact" or those that have very strict editing and publishing standards. Such papers are likely to be written well.

    b.   Read the papers carefully and determine whether they are well written.
Verify that the papers are written clearly. You may be more capable of determining this if they are within your field of expertise, though, at times, the opposite may be the case: if you understand the topic, you may not notice the writing's deficiencies. By contrast, a well-written paper in a field that is unfamiliar to you may clarify things you did not know about that field.

    c.   If possible, determine whether or not these papers have been written by native speakers of English. One way of doing this involves seeking the help of someone who is a native speaker or who has mastered the English language to that level. Note that this may be very difficult to achieve. Note also that even native speakers may have limited writing proficiency.

Select and annotate expressions that convey messages that are important and valuable to you and to your work. Consider words or sentences that may be helpful to you in writing about your work. There are various ways to annotate selected text. You can manually underline or highlight it, or you can use XML-type tag pairs, such as <introduction> ... </introduction>; <method> ... </method>; and the like.

Remember, you cannot copy text verbatim; that would result in plagiarism. The goal is to identify generic parts that can help you produce your own phrases and sentences.

Step 1a Deconstructed We have selected the paper "Social Networking" [14] published in the journal Computer. This journal is published by the IEEE Computer Society, a well-known computer science professional society.

In addition to the abstract, we include here the keywords listed by the authors, an important part of any scientific paper today. These keywords are used for systematic classification and literature review and are helpful in searching for related research topics in publications.

Abstract: In the context of today's electronic media, social networking has come to mean individuals using the Internet and Web applications to communicate in previously impossible ways. This is largely the result of a culture-wide paradigm shift in the uses and possibilities of the Internet itself. The current Web is a much different entity than the Web of a decade ago. This new focus creates a riper breeding ground for social networking and collaboration. In an abstract sense, social networking is about everyone. The mass adoption of social-networking Websites points to an evolution in human social interaction. **Keywords:** Internet; Web sites; groupware; social sciences computing; Internet; Web applications; Web sites; electronic media; human social interaction; social networking; Collaboration; Context; Educational institutions; Explosions; Facebook; Humans; IP networks; Internet; Social network services; Web sites; Facebook; MySpace; Wikipedia; YouTube; how things work; social networking, **URL:** http://tinyurl.com/kmsm7y6

Step 1b Deconstructed We selected a sample abstract, determined that it was well written, and then examined the abstract. The first sentence in the abstract defines the term "social networking," explains what it means, and sets the background by explaining how social networking is used to communicate nowadays.

> *"In the context of today's electronic media, social networking has come to mean individuals using the Internet and Web applications to communicate in previously impossible ways."*

Step 2 Compile the fragments and sentences, clearly marking the "reusable" parts. Reusable parts include those fragments that are generic, that lack specific information. When specific information is removed from the fragments, it leaves gaps that can be filled in. We refer to the removed fragments as "non-reusable" parts. This approach should become part of your learning process — never stop doing it.

Step 2 Deconstructed Using the same text as above, let us remove specific lexical items, so we end up with a generic sentence. We show this process in the text below. In (i), the segments removed are crossed out and the generic parts are left intact. In (ii), the crossed out parts are shown with X to represent the gaps that can be filled in with your own terms or words.

> i "In the context of today's electronic media, social networking has come to mean ~~individuals using the Internet and Web applications~~ to communicate in previously impossible ways."
>
> ii "In the context of today's X, X has come to mean X using X to communicate in previously impossible ways."

This generic sentence is now added to the corpus. It now includes the highlighted text and the gaps, represented by the underlined Xs.

Step 3 ~~Classify the fragments/sentences as belonging to the typical components of a scientific paper, described in Chapter 2.~~

In this third step, we can use two strategies. The first involves assigning the expressions to the pre-defined components of a paper. For example, a fragment selected from the Introduction is automatically labeled as part of the introduction section. This strategy has the advantage of being quick and easy. Its disadvantage is that the user does not get to "reshuffle" the text. The second strategy is to select a large number of fragments (hundreds!), collect them, and then to classify them later. This has the advantage of forcing you to learn how to reuse the text, but requires more time.

Step 3 Deconstructed The generic sentence that was added to the corpus is annotated. It came from an abstract. It can be labeled as **Introduction** or **Abstract**. That is, it can be used as a sample to write a similar sentence in either an abstract or an introduction. It provides **background information**.

Step 4 Practice filling in the gaps with your own material and/ or material based on other examples. For instance, the generic sentence "This X [verb] the X " can become one of these two options, with the underlined words filling in the gaps:

1. This *paper* addresses the *problem*
2. This *letter* analyzes the *case*

Step 4 Deconstructed Using the same text as above, let us fill in the gaps with our own terms or words. See the newly inserted words underlined.

> "In the context of today's X , X has come to mean X using X to communicate in previously impossible ways."

> "In the context of today's *technology, an app* has come to mean *a computer application* using *a mobile platform* to communicate in previously impossible ways."

Now we have a new sentence based on the original stripped-down sentence. This sentence can be added to the corpus and can be used to create a new abstract.

Step 5 Start playing with the pieces, identifying different combinations that appear in the original texts. Create your own combinations — the bricks are the same, but the houses will be different. Throughout this process, try to enrich the possibilities by selecting various fragments (Step 2), and keep filling in the gaps (Step 4).
Here you will create new sentences with new words and terms.

Step 5 Deconstructed To illustrate this step (and the ones that follow), we will "create" an abstract using annotated segments as shown in the previous steps. Our goal is to build our "own" abstract that includes these components and describes the ideas listed next to said components.

- **Background:** Diseases or methods that are difficult to identify.

- **Purpose:** Produce/generate/obtain a highly sensitive and selective sensor.

- **Results:** Nanofilms support the proper architecture/ structure for highly sensitive sensors. Microfluidics is also used.

- **Conclusion:** Impact on other areas.

To show the process, we retrieved a few abstracts from prestigious journals on the topic of biosensors. After having examined these abstracts, we marked parts that could fit into our planned abstract (Step 2). Below we list six text segments with crossed out fragments that have been labeled accordingly. Remember, only the parts that are not crossed out can be reused or imitated.

1. ~~Self-replicating molecules~~ are likely to have played an important role in the ~~origin of life,~~ and a small number of ~~fully synthetic self-replicators~~ have already been ~~described.~~ Yet it remains an open question which factors most effectively ~~bias the replication toward the far-from-equilibrium distributions characterizing even simple organisms.~~ (Background and gap) [15].

2. We detected the temporal ~~order of their enzymatic incorporation into a growing DNA strand~~ with ~~zero-mode waveguide~~ nanostructure arrays, which provide ~~optical observation volume confinement and~~ enable parallel, simultaneous detection of ~~thousands of single-molecule sequencing reactions.~~ (Results) [16].

3. The ~~squeezing of polymers in narrow gaps~~ is important for the ~~dynamics of nanostructure~~ fabrication by ~~nanoimprint embossing and~~ the operation of ~~polymer boundary lubricants.~~ (Methods) [17].

4. We developed a biosensor to study ~~the subcellular distribution of phosphatidylserine~~ and found that ~~it binds the cytosolic leaflets of the plasma membrane, as well as endosomes and lysosomes.~~ (Methods + Results) [18].

5. The high sensitivity of ~~back-scattering interferometry and~~ small volumes of microfluidics allowed the ~~entire calmodulin~~ assay to be performed with ~~200 picomoles of solute.~~ (Results + Conclusion) [19].

6. Because it is similar to ~~10,000~~ times more sensitive than previous ~~CEST~~ methods and other ~~molecular magnetic resonance imaging~~ techniques, it marks a critical step toward the application ~~of xenon biosensors~~ as selective ~~contrast agents in biomedical applications.~~ (Conclusion), [20].

Step 6 Start over again with the selected expressions, now classifying them according to rhetorical messages (e.g., describe, contrast, confirm, define, compare, introduce, etc.). The idea is to have a collection of expressions that you can draw from as you wish to state specific contents. Continue selecting additional expressions and filling in the gaps.

Step 6 Deconstructed Our segments now look like the ones below, with the additional labels listed at the end [inside square brackets].

1. *X* are likely to have played an important role in the *X*, and a small number of *X* have already been *X*. Yet it

remains an open question which factors most effectively X. (Background and gap) [15] [Introduce].

2. We detected the temporal X with X nanostructure arrays, which provide X enable parallel, simultaneous detection of X. (Results) [16] [Describe].

3. The X is important for the X fabrication by X the operation of X. (Methods) [21] [Highlight importance].

Step 7 Start working with full text passages, rather than only with individual sentences. Repeat the process of combining pieces, as in Step 5. Now is the time to learn to use connectives efficiently. Compile a list of expressions including *however, in contrast, indeed, on the other hand, furthermore, nevertheless, since, because,* etc. and identify the ones that appear in the sentences you selected. In the segments of text listed in Step 5, item 6 contains "because."

Step 8 It is time to produce a full section of a paper. Select the subcomponents, and implement them by reusing material from your earlier practices. Fill in the gaps, for which help may be obtained by retrieving material from the practices. Pay attention to the use of connectives and the coherence of the text.

Step 8 Deconstructed Pay attention to how each segment is written, following the segments from the corpus:

1. X are likely to have played an important role in the X, and a small number of X have already been X. Yet it remains an open question which factors most effectively X. (Background and gap) [15].
   ⇒ *Chagas' disease* is likely to have been one of the most important *neglected diseases*, and a small number of

methods have already been *developed to detect it.* Yet it remains an open question which factors most *affect the detection.* (Background and gap).

2. We detected the temporal *X* with *X* nanostructure arrays, which provide *X* enable parallel, simultaneous detection of *X* . (Results) [16] [Describe].
⇒ We detected the *presence of antibodies against T. Cruzi* with nanostructured films, which provide *molecular recognition processes* and enable parallel, simultaneous detection of *Chagas' disease and Leishmaniasis.* (Results).

3. The *X* is important for the *X* fabrication by *X* the operation of *X* . (Methods) [17] [Highlight importance].
⇒ The *organization of polymeric nanostructured films has been exploited in* the fabrication *of sensing units by the layer-by-layer technique.* (Methods)

4. We developed a biosensor to study X and found that *X* . (Methods + Results) [18].
⇒ We developed a biosensor *array to detect antibodies in the nanomolar range,* and found *that the array is also selective for the Chagas' disease.* (Methods + Results)

5. The high sensitivity of *X* small volumes of microfluidics allowed the *X* assay to be performed with X. (Results + Conclusion) [19].
⇒ The high sensitivity of *the detection method and* small volumes of microfluidics allowed *the entire* assay to be performed *within a few seconds.*
(Results + Conclusion)

6. Because *X* is similar to *X* times more sensitive than previous *X* , it marks a critical step toward the application of X biosensors as selective X. (Conclusion) [20].
⇒ Because *the sensor array* is similar to *1,000* times more sensitive than previous *sensors*, it marks a critical step

toward the application of *molecular recognition-based* biosensors as selective *elements in clinical diagnosis.*

Now we list all of these newly created segments:

1. Chagas' disease is likely to have been one of the most important neglected diseases, and a small number of methods have already been developed to detect it. Yet it remains an open question which factors most affect the detection.

2. We detected the presence of antibodies against T. Cruzi with nanostructured films, which provide molecular recognition processes and enable parallel, simultaneous detection of Chagas' disease and Leishmaniasis.

3. The organization of polymeric nanostructured films has been exploited in the fabrication of sensing units by the layer-by-layer technique.

4. We developed a biosensor array to detect antibodies in the nanomolar range, and found that the array is also selective for the Chagas' disease.

5. The high sensitivity of the detection method and small volumes of microfluidics allowed the entire assay to be performed within a few seconds.

6. Because the sensor array is similar to 1,000 times more sensitive than previous sensors, it marks a critical step toward the application of molecular recognition-based biosensors as selective elements in clinical diagnosis.

We switch the text in Parts 2 and 3. Our abstract now looks like this:

Chagas' disease is likely to have been one of the most important neglected diseases, and a small number of methods have already been developed to detect it. Yet it remains an open question which factors most affect the detection. The organization of polymeric nanostructured films has been exploited in the fabrication of sensing units by the layer-by-layer technique. We detected the presence of antibodies against T. Cruzi with nanostructured films, which provide molecular recognition processes and enable parallel, simultaneous detection of Chagas' disease and Leishmaniasis. We developed a biosensor array to detect antibodies in the nanomolar range, and found that the array is also selective for the Chagas' disease. The high sensitivity of the detection method and small volumes of microfluidics allowed the entire assay to be performed within a few seconds. Because the sensor array is similar to 1,000 times more sensitive than previous sensors, it marks a critical step toward the application of molecular recognition-based biosensors as selective elements in clinical diagnosis.

Step 9 Edit the text. Check the section for typos and other surface errors. Eliminate unnecessary words. Check the consistency of the subcomponents and their interrelationship. Analyze the contents for completeness and accuracy.

Step 9 Deconstructed We must edit the text to make it coherent.

Chagas' disease is likely to be one of the most important neglected diseases, and a small number of methods have already been developed to detect it. Yet it remains an open question which factors most affect the detection. In this study, the organization of polymeric nanostructured films has been exploited in the fabrication of sensing units by the layer-by-layer technique. With this methodology, we developed a biosensor array to detect the presence of antibodies against T. Cruzi with nanostructured films, which provide molecular recognition processes and enable parallel, simultaneous detection of Chagas' disease and

Leishmaniasis. We detected antibodies in the nanomolar range, and found that the array is also selective for the Chagas' disease. The high sensitivity of the detection method and small volumes of microfluidics allowed the entire assay to be performed within a few seconds. Because the sensor array is similar to 1,000 times more sensitive than previous sensors, it marks a critical step toward the application of molecular recognition-based biosensors as selective elements in clinical diagnosis.

One more pass!

Chagas' disease is ~~likely to be~~ one of the most ~~important~~ neglected diseases, ~~and a small number of~~ with few methods ~~have already been developed~~ available to detect it. Yet it remains an open question which factors ~~most~~ primarily affect ~~the~~ its detection. In this study, the organization of polymeric nanostructured films has been ~~exploited~~ used in the fabrication of sensing units by the layer-by-layer technique. ~~With~~ Using this method, we developed a biosensor array to detect the presence of antibodies against T. Cruzi with nanostructured films, which provide molecular recognition processes and enable parallel, simultaneous detection of Chagas' disease and Leishmaniasis. We detected antibodies in the nanomolar range, and found that the array is also selective for Chagas' disease. The high sensitivity of the detection method and small volumes of microfluidics allowed the entire assay to be performed within a few seconds. ~~Because the sensor array is~~ similar to 1,000 times more sensitive than previous sensors, it marks a critical step toward the application of molecular recognition-based biosensors as selective elements in clinical diagnosis.

Edited, again; one more pass — this process continues.

Chagas' disease is one of the most neglected with few methods available to detect it. Yet it remains an open question which factors primarily affect its detection. In this study, we

focus on detection by examining the **structure** of polymeric nanostructured films that have been **used to produce** sensing units using the layer-by-layer technique. We developed a biosensor array to detect the presence of antibodies against T. Cruzi with nanostructured films, which provide molecular recognition processes and enable parallel, simultaneous detection of Chagas' disease and Leishmaniasis. We detected antibodies in the nanomolar range and found that the array is also selective for Chagas' disease. The high sensitivity of the detection method and small volumes of microfluidics allowed the entire assay to be performed in a few seconds. **Our results**, close to 1,000 times more sensitive than previous sensors, mark a critical step toward the application of molecular recognition-based biosensors as selective elements in clinical diagnosis.

There is no doubt that if you follow these steps, you will eventually develop the facility to write easily flowing and clear text.

An alternative to this tedious manual annotation process is to let a computer do some of the work. We now describe two tools that we have developed, which can make the annotation process a little less tedious

3.3 AUTOMATIC ANNOTATION

Aluísio and collaborators have developed two tools that use machine learning to annotate the components of abstracts in English: *AZEA-WEB*[1] ("Argumentative Zoning for English Abstracts") [22] and *MAZEA-WEB*[2] ("Multi-label Argumentative Zoning for English Abstracts") [23]. These tools annotate text automatically, tagging each sentence with a label. A sentence may have more than one label.

AZEA-WEB, however, can only assign a single label to a chosen unit. Usually, the unit to be annotated is a sentence.

---

[1] http://www.nilc.icmc.usp.br/azea-web/

[2] http://www.nilc.icmc.usp.br/mazea-web/

Alternatively, it is possible to choose smaller ("segments") or larger ("zones") units.

Two approaches have been proposed to automatically detect moves in scientific texts. One is the Argumentative Zoner [22, 24, 25, 26]. This linguistically-rich approach uses lexical, syntactic, and structural features, such as the first formulaic expression found in the sentence, the presence of auxiliary modal verbs, and the position of a sentence within the text, respectively. The approach has been used to annotate zones, sentences, or segments of a sentence. The definition of argumentative zones is given by the sentential-rhetorical speech act of single, important sentences — landmark sentences, e.g., "in this paper we develop a method for," or "in contrast to [reference], our approach uses ..." Zones are useful when annotating an entire paper because they enable us to use a small set of labels to annotate large segments of text. However, an abstract annotated with segments is better because it enables us to combine clauses with different labels in order to create a short abstract. Small-segment annotation would require an automatic parser, which is inferior in performance compared to a simple sentence segmentation tool.

MAZEA-WEB, on the other hand, was developed to identify rhetorical moves in abstracts. More specifically, it was designed to (i) overcome the limitations of assigning only one class label (a move, in our case); and (ii) to use very small training corpora (of up to 100 documents), commonly used in automatic classifiers. Sentence-level annotation is common in scientific papers. It is computationally cheaper to automatically segment sentences than smaller units.

The two sentences in Figure 3.1 were taken from the corpus used to train MAZEA. They illustrate the use of a single label to annotate one sentence and three labels to annotate the second sentence, that is, multilabel annotation.

> **\<background\>** Insulin is a unique model system in which to study protein fibrillization, since its three disulfide bridges are retained in the fibrillar state and thus limit the conformational space available to the polypeptide chains during misfolding and fibrillization . **\</background\>**
> **\<background\>** Taking into account this unique conformational restriction, **\</background\>**
> **\<purpose\>** we modeled possible monomeric subunits of the insulin amyloid fibrils **\</purpose\>**
> **\<method\>** using β-solenoid folds, namely, the β-helix and β-roll . **\</method\>**

Figure 3.1: Examples of monolabel and multilabel annotation of sentences.

The annotation in Figure 3.1 uses the XML format.

In the first sentence, the (\<background\> ... \</background\>) tag pair indicates the context of the study, any reference to previous work, relevance of the topic, and main motivations behind the study. The second sentence is annotated with multiple labels, using three sets of tags:

1. Giving the context (\<background\> ... \</background\>);
2. Describing the intended aims of the paper or hypotheses (\<purpose\> ...
   \</purpose\>); and
3. Describing the methods and the materials used in the study (\<method\>
   ... \</method\>).

3.3.1 ANNOTATION GUIDELINES

The systems that use automatic annotation required training. Three experienced annotators discussed ten abstracts taken from the two broad research fields: (i) Life and Health Science (LH) and (ii) Physical Sciences and Engineering (PE). They verified the reliability of the multi-label sentence classification. To do this, we selected abstracts from each discipline: 38 from the PE corpus and 34 from the LH corpus. We developed a list to annotate these abstracts using six main components and subcomponents, see Figure 3.2.

1. Background
    1.1 Context, justification, and explanations
    1.2 Literature review and previous studies
    1.3 Topic relevance
2. Gap: What is missing in the literature
3. Purpose
    3.1 Objectives
    3.2 Hypothesis
4. Method
    4.1 Description of the methods
    4.2 Data description
    4.3 Indication that the methods will be described
    4.4 Indication that the methods, problems and/or limitations will be discussed
5. Results
    5.1 Description of the results
    5.2 Interpretation or discussion of the results
    5.3 Hypotheses obtained from the presented results
    5.4 Speculation about the results
6. Conclusion
    6.1 Conclusions

6.2 Recommendations, suggestions, and opinions

6.3 Future work

6.4 Contributions and applications

6.5 Discussion of possible interpretations and/or applications of the results

6.6 Discussion of the limitations of the work or indication that those limitations will be discussed

Figure 3.2: Scheme used to annotate abstracts in AZEA

The human annotators verified AZEA's annotation. They followed the scheme shown in Fig. 3.2 to characterize each component:

1. Background — the context of the study, including any reference to previous work on the topic, relevance of the topic, and the main motivations behind the study;

2. Gap — any indication that the researched topic has not been explored, that little is known about it, or that previous attempts to overcome a given problem or issue have been unsuccessful;

3. Purpose — the intended aims of the paper or hypotheses;

4. Methods — the procedures adopted as well as the description of the data and materials used in the study;

5. Result — the main findings or, in some cases, the indication that the findings will be described or discussed, and discussion or interpretation of the findings, which includes any hypothesis raised as a result of the findings presented in the paper; and

6. Conclusion — the general conclusion of the paper, subjective opinions about the results, suggestions, and recommendations for future work.

This verification process required changing labels and correcting errors that resulted from the segmentation of sentence boundaries. Annotators were also able to assign more than one label to a given sentence, whenever it was appropriate.

3.3.2 A SIMPLE, FAST, AND RELIABLE ANNOTATION PROCEDURE

Since our primary goal was to build a classifier to assign as many labels as possible to a given sentence, our initial challenge was to decide when and how to segment sentences. First we randomly selected five abstracts from each corpus and used a full syntactic parsing (OpenNLP project) to divide all sentences into either prepositional phrases or clauses. We then used a script to identify clauses and prepositional phrases related to the task.

We allowed the annotators to use their own judgment in deciding whether or not to segment sentences and how to do so. In the case of components that span several sentences, we repeated the same label over all sentences. This approach facilitated the annotation process and allowed us to capture the granularity of the segmentation process.

We demonstrate how to use MAZEA-WEB in Chapter 5.

3.4 IN SUMMARY

In this chapter we have:

1. learned an efficient way to quickly go through a lot of publications to determine which ones are worthy of our time, and how to read through those effectively;

2. studied and demonstrated a nine-step method to annotate texts manually, establish a collection of "reusable" text parts, and construct originally written text around those reusable parts;

3. learned about two tools that provide automatic annotation capabilities to ease the manual effort of the learn-by-example annotation technique.

Chapter 4

Stella E.O. Tagnin

Using Corpus Linguistics to Overcome the Language Barrier

IN THIS CHAPTER WE WILL LEARN:

1. What makes a phrase or text sound natural

2. How to recognize a natural vs. an unnatural phrase/text

3. How to write natural/fluent text

4. How to use tools that can help us write better text

We begin with an overview of conventionality in language, that is, the usual way of expressing oneself, and introduce its various categories with a wealth of examples. Because conventional items are more pervasive in language than one would expect, it is important that anyone wishing to produce a natural text be familiar with these linguistic expressions. One way to identify them quickly is by utilizing Corpus Linguistics, which relies on the observation of large chunks of authentic language by means of specific corpus analysis tools. These tools allow us to examine vocabulary in context. In section two, we introduce Corpus Linguistics and show how to use it. In section three, we show how to build a customized corpus and how to extract a relevant vocabulary to build a glossary specific to your area.

4.1 WHAT IS CONVENTIONALITY IN LANGUAGE?

Contrary to common belief, a very large part of language is not compositional, which means that it is not created on the spur of the moment. Rather, it is made up of prefabricated chunks, that is, fixed or semi-fixed combinations of words. Mastering these chunks and using them appropriately is what makes a language sound natural and fluent.

There are many different kinds of chunks. Let us look at them.

4.2 COLLIGATIONS

These are combinations of words with a grammatical category, like prepositions, verbs, adjectives, etc. Usually these do not pose a problem because we learn most of them when we study grammar. Here are a few examples:

- *LOOK*[3] + *preposition* = *look **at**, look **for***
- *BELIEVE* + *THAT clause* = They **believe that** some explanations and methods are better than others.[4]
- *TRY* + *TO infinitive* = We could **try to turn** 7-ketocholesterol back into native cholesterol.
- *HELP* + *PERSONAL PRONOUN* + *(TO) INFINITIVE* = The outline below will **help you (to) organize** your thoughts and write a good paper.
- *PREPOSITION* + *HELP-ing* = We thank our colleagues for ***helping*** to collect data during this study.

4.3 COLLOCATIONS

In every language, there are expressions that are strung together and are used as a "unit." These units will always sound "right" to a native speaker. For instance, in English you "dream about" something, whereas the "equivalent" in Spanish or Portuguese translates to "dream with" something. These units are called **collocations**. There are various types of collocations: *verbal*, *nominal*, *adjectival*, and *adverbial*. Let us examine each one.

---

[3] Words in SMALL CAPS indicate lemmatized forms, that is, they stand for any form of the word. In the case of verbs, they stand for all tenses and persons of that verb; in the case of nouns they stand for both singular and plural.

[4] All examples are extracted from the Contemporary Corpus of American English — COCA (www.americancorpus.org) and only slightly adapted when needed.

4.3.1 VERBAL COLLOCATIONS

Certain nouns are used with specific verbs. These nouns can either be the subject or the object of the verb. In the examples below, you will see that a river flows, a study is conducted, and research is done:

- $N[subj] + V$ = The canyon-carving Colorado **River flows** into the upper reaches of Lake Mead.
- $V + N[obj]$ = The team recently **conducted** a **study** of forty-two sites where tigers are still found.
- Did you **do** any **research** for the book?

4.3.2 NOMINAL COLLOCATIONS

These are something like compound nouns. Most of them are formed by $N + N$:

- It's an incredible **case study** about the role of the court.
- There is little **research data** related to obesity and THR.

but $N + of + N$ also occurs:

- Line's **point of view** was based on his research that found limited commonality in journal rankings...
- From the patient's **point of view**, they are likely to have little expectation that you can solve their problem.
- A one-way **analysis of variance** (ANOVA) showed that there was no gender difference in PGU or in...
- We used a two-way **analysis of variance** (funding source x program participation) to determine whether...
- **Locus of control** is the degree to which people perceive positive or negative events as being...
- There is limited evidence that external **locus of control** is related to underachievement.

The names of many institutions follow this pattern:

- Data from the Texas **Department of Agriculture** shows about one in five inspected stores...
- ... a clinical geneticist and neurobiologist at the Duke University **School of Medicine**
- ... a biologist at the Georgia **Institute of Technology**.
- Our project would be a pilot for our **board of education**.
- The **Department of Health** is launching a campaign to raise awareness about the symptoms of lung cancer.

4.3.3 ADJECTIVAL COLLOCATIONS

Nouns may also combine preferably with certain adjectives. These combinations are called adjectival collocations. For example, when you refer to the study you are conducting you may either say *present study* or *current study*. Here are some examples:

- The *present study* employed both elicited and spontaneous language measures.
- Only the measures relevant to the *current study* are reported here.
- They conducted a **longitudinal study** of 54 children from first through fourth grades.
- We illustrate how to list **raw data** using an efficient coding system.
- The study also employed a coding team for analysis of the **qualitative data**.
- The parameter values for the simulation were derived from **empirical data**.

4.3.4 ADVERBIAL COLLOCATIONS

Again, some verbs and adjectives combine more frequently with certain adverbs. These adverbs may precede or follow the verb or adjective, but usually the order is fixed.

- He had **fairly extensive** knowledge of the colonies and their operation.
- You've done some **fairly extensive** research on this.
- This study demonstrates a **statistically significant** association of serum PCB levels with increased diabetes prevalence overall.
- We detected small, but **statistically significant** heterogeneity in the risk of mortality between census tracts.
- The only **widely acknowledged** contraindication of IO access is fracture of the bone.
- Although **widely acknowledged** among traditional cultures, sleep paralysis is one of the most...
- Many variations of this procedure have been reported in the literature, with **widely divergent** success rates.
- Many who have used other systems have **widely divergent** reactions toward HMOs.

Here is a case in which the order is not fixed:

- Areas with overlapping high values could be **carefully studied** through risk assessment.
- The team **carefully studied** every part of the virus.
- I'm **carefully studying** my setup and becoming very familiar with it.
- This material should be approached with an open mind, **studied carefully** and critically considered.
- The question would have to be **studied carefully** first.
- And, in fact, economists have **studied** this **carefully**.

4.4 Binomials

These are formed of two words belonging to the same grammatical category, for example, verbs, nouns, or adjectives, linked by a conjunction or preposition. They can be reversible, meaning that the order can be inverted, as in *social or political* or *political or social*, or irreversible, in which the order is fixed, as in *come and go* or *better or worse*. It is important to make sure you know whether a binomial is reversible or irreversible. Further ahead we will see how you can find this information. In the meantime, here are some contextualized examples of irreversible binomials:

N and *N*

- That's the kind of **research and development** that is being worked on by the space program.
- Nokia said it will shut some **research and development** projects.
- He had always been involved in **science and technology**.
- It's a chance to see women at work in **science and technology**.

V and *V*

- Smokers can be reassured that even if they have **tried and failed** to quit using NRT, there is nothing to stop them trying again.
- Lawmakers have **tried and failed** to regulate the flow of objectionable material through the Internet.

V or *V*

- This interaction could **increase or decrease** the rate of a biochemical reaction.

- More importantly, fat regulates itself by producing adipokines that can **increase or decrease** appetite and metabolic rate.

N or N

- Statistics are inadequate to conclude whether the past decade has been a **success or failure**.
- The authors suggest that patient selection may play a role in determining the **success or failure** of treatment.

Adj and Adj

- Data on **positive and negative** malaria tests conducted in Ontario were used to assign persons to 1 of 2 groups.
- It becomes more interesting when the **positive and negative** rotating motions differ in amplitude.

Adj or Adj

- Your chances of being **overweight or obese** increase half a percent with every friend in your network who is obese.

- Nearly 17% of U.S. kids are considered **overweight or obese**.

Just a few examples of reversible binomials:

- Most of the parents, **black or white**, would be mortified when they got the teacher's note.
- A map doesn't know if a community is **black or white**, rich or poor, Democratic or Republican.
- Young Latinas are more likely to be teen parents than their **white or black** counterparts.
- They couldn't tell if I was **white or black**, a boy or a girl.
- Whether it's due to **physical or mental** inability is irrelevant.

- These drugs may cause **physical or mental** dependence when taken over long periods.
- Indicators of socioeconomic deprivation have been linked to **mental or physical** health deficits.
- This is especially true for seniors who suffer from **mental or physical** infirmities.

In addition to these fairly clear-cut categories, there are longer structures, which we chose to call *conventional expressions*.

4.5 CONVENTIONAL EXPRESSIONS

These are not to be confused with idiomatic expressions. The meaning of idiomatic expressions is not transparent, that is, you cannot understand it unless you have learned it as a whole. One classical example is *kick the bucket*, which does not mean that someone kicked a bucket, but rather that somebody died. By contrast, the meaning of conventional expressions is quite literal. For example, *fit for human consumption* means exactly that — the product referred to is fit (= adequate) to be consumed by humans. Many such expressions are typical of scientific writing. In the examples below, *Det* stands for *Determiner* and may represent an article (*a, an, the*), a demonstrative (*this, that, these, those*), or even an adjective preceded by an article (*the other, a recent*, etc.):

Det + study shows/showed that

- The other **study showed that** both the occurrence of recurring ear infections...
- A recent **study showed that** women outnumber men as students at every degree level...
- The present **study shows that** bimodal benefit is greater for the listeners with...

Det + study reported (that)

- One **study reported that** exercisers who took fish-oil supplements lost more fat and gained...
- The **study reported** in this article addresses this research gap, focusing on ...

Det + results suggest that

- Some **results suggest that** the strength of the lexicon-syntax association is sensitive to modality.
- These **results suggest that** future prevention efforts within the DR context should take...

Results + indicated (that)

- **Results indicated that** the intervention was functionally related to increases in...
- The **results indicated**, however, no significant difference between men and women in the perceived intensity...

FILL/ADDRESS the/this gap/void in the literature

- The current experiment sought to **fill this gap in the literature**.
- ... and **fill the gap in the literature** by building on prior works in several important ways.
- It begins to **fill the gap in the literature** regarding...
- This paper attempts to **fill this void in the literature**...
- Our aim was to **address these** critical **gaps in the literature**.
- To **address this gap in the literature**, we used an objective...
- We were interested in **addressing this gap in the literature** by examining...
- In this study, I **addressed a gap in the literature**...

- The objective of the current study was to **address the gap in the literature** pertaining to...

X not (BE) previously V-ed in the literature

- New findings **not previously** reported **in the literature** emerged from the study.
- ...a finding **not previously** identified **in the literature**.
- ...**not previously** addressed **in the literature**.
- Such a long-term investigation **has not been previously** described **in the literature**.
- ...paranasal sinuses **has not been previously** discussed **in the literature**.
- ...has **not been previously** recognized **in the literature**.

X (BE) previously V-ed in the literature

- These ideas shed light on a gray area **previously** ignored **in the literature**
- The majority of these competencies have been **previously** identified **in the literature** as important...
- Only 28 cases have been **previously** reported **in the literature**.
- As **previously** noted **in the literature**, teacher ratings...

(Det) results suggest/showed/indicate(d) (that)

- These **results suggest** that future prevention efforts within the DR context should take into account...
- Our **results suggest** that interventions implemented during the last 3 decades have been effective at...
- These **results suggest** a pattern of inequality in tropical health outcomes in Ontario with...
- **Results suggest** that tasks aiming to differentiate the two groups should be...

- **Results showed** that there were no significant differences in variance between the groups...
- The **results showed** that the distal axon count actually increased with the 2.5:1 nerve ratio.
- **Results indicated** that the data generated during secondary prevention...
- The **results indicated** no differences in categorical perception.
- Our **results indicate** that Hie and Hif share many features characteristic of invasive ncHi disease.
- **Results indicate** that all three variables, number of time points, residual, and methods...

Although idiomatic expressions are part of the conventional items that make up language, they are not very recurrent in scientific writing, which tends to be more formal.

4.6 CORPUS LINGUISTICS

Corpus Linguistics is based on the assumption that language is probabilistic, that is, that certain combinations of words have a higher probability of occurring than others, although these other ones may be perfectly grammatical. Taking a few of the examples above, why should *increase or decrease* be more recurrent than *decrease or increase*? Why is *results suggest* much more frequent than *results suggested* in academic language? Why is *fill the gap* preferred to *bridge the gap* in academic discourse although the latter is recurrent in everyday language? The answer has actually been given above: language has conventionalized it that way.

Now, how can we find out what is conventional in language? By resorting to Corpus Linguistics. Corpus Linguistics relies on investigating a large body of texts — called a *corpus* — to retrieve its results. But a corpus is not any collection of texts; it has to be compiled according to certain criteria, which depend on the purpose of the investigation.[5] Fortunately there are various ready-made corpora available online that can be freely investigated using their built-in tools. Some of these corpora are:

- **COCA — Corpus of Contemporary American English.**[6] This corpus has over 460 million words, with texts ranging from 1990 to the current year (they are updated annually). They cover a variety of genres, from spoken language and fiction to journalistic and academic. As the corpus is tagged for part-of-speech (POS-tagged) — that is, each word has a label indicating its grammatical category — users can search not only for words, but also for parts-of-speech. For example, *present* only as a verb or *study* only as a noun. We give examples of possible queries below.

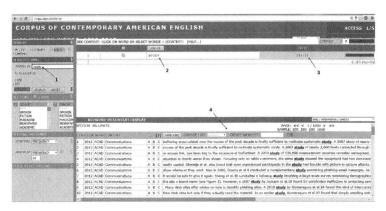

Figure 4.1: Screenshot for the word *study* in COCA.

---

[5] In the next section, we will discuss the criteria to build a customized corpus and the stand-alone tools necessary to investigate it.
[6] www.americancorpus.org

- **BNC-BYU — British National Corpus**[7].This corpus is made available by the Brigham Young University. It contains 100 million words, spanning texts from the 1980s to 1993. It is also POS-tagged and has the same interface as the COCA. One must remember that no texts after 1993 are included so, for example, a search for *scanner* would probably yield no results because it had not been invented at that time.

The main tool available on both sites is a **concordancer**, which brings you ALL occurrences in the corpus of the word you are studying. This is called a KWIC (Keyword In Context) concordance, because the word is shown in context, which is not necessarily a complete sentence. However, a larger portion of the context may be obtained by clicking on the concordance line.

In the screenshot in Fig. 4.1, you see the word *study* (1) in the box where you insert the word you want to investigate. On the upper right-hand side, you see the result — in this case the word *study* (2) and the number of occurrences in the corpus (3), that is, it occurs 144,743 times. By clicking on the word (2), you will get the contexts in which it occurs (4). These are the concordance lines. On the left-hand side of the contexts, you get the source from which the example was taken. In this case, all of them come from academic texts that deal with communications and are dated 2012.

As the corpus is POS-tagged, you can carry out more sophisticated queries. So, for example, if you want to know with which verbs *study* co-occurs, or, in other words, if you want to find out the verbal collocations for *study*, you can refine your search. Look at the next screenshot (Fig. 4.2):

---

[7] corpus.byu.edu/bnc/

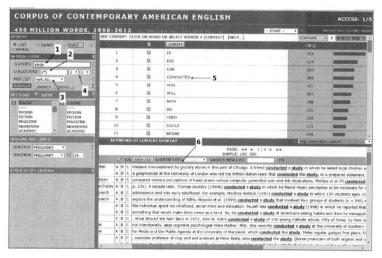

Figure 4.2: Screenshot of a search for *study* preceded by a verb (1 or 2 words to the left).

After inserting *study* again in the WORD(S) box (1), you can specify the category you want your search word to co-occur with. In this case, we inserted [v*], which stands for any verb (2). In fact, when you click on COLLOCATES and then on POS LIST, and choose verb.ALL (3) from the drop-down list, the COLLOCATES box is completed automatically. Finally, you can also establish the position in which you want your verb to occur. In (4) we have inserted 2 in the left box, which means the verb will occur 1 or 2 positions before the search word. If we had inserted 2 in the right box, the verb would occur 1 or 2 positions to the right of *study*. The results show the list of verbs that occur in the position(s) we have specified. Among them, we identify *conducted* as a frequent collocate, which would give us the verbal collocation *conducted a study*. If we go farther down in the list, we will come to *conduct* in position 20 with 117 occurrences, while *conducted* shows 348 occurrences. This also tells us that *conducted a study* is twice as common as *conduct a study*. In other words, the collocation occurs more frequently in its past form.

Table 4.1 shows the first 20 verbs that occur 1 or 2 positions to the right of *study*. As we can see, *conducted* is there again. But other verbs are related to what the *study* investigated, that is, what the study *showed/shows/suggests*, etc. An examination of the concordance lines for each verb will help establish the exact context in which the collocation is customarily used.

		CONTEXT	FREQ	
1		WAS	7175	
2		IS	3464	
3		WERE	2530	
4		FOUND	2398	
5		CONDUCTED	1487	
6		HAS	1162	
7		ARE	1109	
8		SHOWED	927	
9		PUBLISHED	882	
10		BE	812	
11		EXAMINED	737	
12		REPORTED	714	
13		HAD	674	
14		DID	663	
15		SHOWS	559	
16		HAVE	549	
17		WILL	538	
18		SUGGESTS	530	
19		SUGGEST	488	
20		INCLUDED	466	

Table 4.1: Verbs that occur 1 or 2 positions to the right of *study*.

It is quite common for a specific search to bring unexpected results. For instance, looking for the most usual adjectives used with *investigation*, we come across *further*, yielding *further investigation*. However, if we study the concordances another co-occurrence calls our attention: we notice that this collocation occurs frequently with the verb WARRANT:

- These results are consistent with previous findings and **warrant further investigation**...
- ...this observation **warrants further investigation**.
- Because **further investigation** of these treatments is **warranted**, the committee is...
- ...we believe that **further investigation** on this topic is **warranted**.
- This hypothesis **warrants further investigation**.
- This possibility **warrants further investigation**.
- Although **further investigation** is **warranted**, the high prevalence of obesity...
- Its use and applications as a semipermanent injectable agent certainly **warrant further investigation**.
- Although this presents an attractive hypothesis that **warrants further investigation**, the mechanisms...

To make sure that this is really a longer conventional expression, we can carry out a specific search to that end, as shown in the screenshot in Fig. 4.3, where we inserted *further investigation* (1) as the search expression and specified that we want results to show the verb WARRANT (2) in up to 4 positions either to the left or to the right of the expression (3).

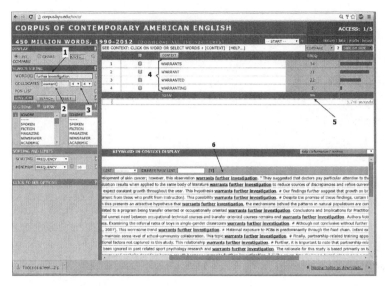

Figure 4.3: Sample concordance lines for *[warrant] further investigation*.

The results show the various forms in which WARRANT occurs (4), yielding a total of 89 occurrences (5). They also indicate that the simple present tense form is more frequent than the past tense: 65 occurrences in the present versus 22 in the past. When we look at the concordance lines we realize that the most recurrent structure is *Det (NP)* WARRANT *further investigation*, as in Table 4.2.

Determiner	Noun Phrase	WARRANT	
This	hypothesis	warrants	further investigation.
This	worrisome	warrants	further investigation.
This	trend x.x	warrants	further investigation.
These	findings x.x	warrant	further investigation.
That		warranted	further investigation.

Table 4.2: COCA results showing various forms in which WARRANT occurs.

However, if we look at the concordances for *warranted*, we will notice that in most examples it stands for the verb in a passive construction:

- ... saying no *further investigation* is **warranted**.
- ... reasonable grounds to believe that *further investigation* is **warranted**.
- *Further investigation* is **warranted** to test the thesis that ...
- ... and found that no *further investigation* was **warranted**.

Once again, looking closer at the concordances with *warranted* we find that it seems to form an even longer conventional expression. In 5 of the 22 concordance lines, we get *reasonable grounds to believe that further investigation is warranted*:

- ... that the Department of Justice finds **no reasonable grounds to believe that further investigation is warranted**.
- ... saying there are **no reasonable grounds to believe that further investigation is warranted**.
- ... if she determines that there are **reasonable grounds to believe that further investigation is warranted**.
- ... the Attorney General concludes that "there are **no reasonable grounds to believe that further investigation is warranted** ... "
- The Attorney General determines that **reasonable grounds** do exist **to believe that further investigation may be warranted**.

Although these online corpora can be very helpful, sometimes your field of work is too specific and these corpora do not have enough material in that domain to answer all of your questions. In that case, a customized corpus has to be built. In the following section, we address the steps to build a representative and balanced corpus as well as the stand-alone tools that must be used to query it.

4.7 BUILDING AND INVESTIGATING A CORPUS

Let us suppose your area of research is Bone Quality. A customized corpus in that domain, if properly built, should present a significant number of the conventional items that characterize it. Let us then see how we should go about building a reliable corpus. First, let us stress that a corpus, for Corpus Linguistics, is a collection of digitized texts, selected according to the researcher's goals, which can be investigated with computational tools such as a concordancer, which we have already seen above.

With this in mind, it seems that the Web might be the best source for retrieving the texts to form the corpus. But things are not that easy. A few decisions have to be made before we start, or a lot of work may be wasted. Here are a few questions to be answered:

1. What kind of texts should be included? Scientific papers? Theses and dissertations? Newspaper articles? Manuals?
2. How many texts of each type should be included?
3. Will there be a limit to the extension of the corpus? What would be considered a "good" size?
4. Should older texts also be included?

In fact, the major question that will help answer all the ones above is "What is the corpus for?" Once the goal has been established, a design can be drawn. Our corpus will help us write papers to be submitted to conferences or journals. Therefore, we may include, for example, texts according to Table 4.3.

Type of text	Number of texts
Articles published in journals	50
Theses and dissertations	10

Table 4.3: Types and number of text

Now we can go to the Web and collect the material. All of it should be stored in its original format, for future reference in case any doubt arises, and in plain text format (.txt), which is usually the format required by the computational tools that will be used.

Any non-linguistic material, such as graphs, tables, figures, URLs, etc., should be discarded. Each text should be given a name to make it easily identifiable. In our case, articles could be named according to the journal they were published in, for instance, JACN1, standing for the first text retrieved from the *Journal of the American College of Nutrition*, or NEJM5, for the fifth article taken from *The New England Journal of Medicine*. Theses and dissertations might be named TH_USP_2012, for instance, standing for a thesis from the University of São Paulo completed in 2012. The information chosen to name the file is up to the researcher to decide.

The next step is to organize the files. In our case we could have one file for "Theses and Dissertations" and another one for "Academic articles." This will allow us to search for these two genres separately, if needed.

Our corpus is now ready to be queried. For that, we need a computational tool. *AntConc* [27] is a free tool.[8] It features the main tools for corpus investigation and is quite easy to use. There is also a tutorial available as a "readme" file. The other one, which may be more suited to more sophisticated research, is *WordSmith Tools*, version 6.0 [28]. It can be purchased at http://www.lexically.net/wordsmith.

---

[8] Available for download from http://www.antlab.sci.waseda.ac.jp/software.html.

We have already seen various examples of concordances from the COCA. In Figure 4.4 we can see another one, from our Bone Quality corpus using AntConc — notice the **Concordance** tab in the upper part of the screen.

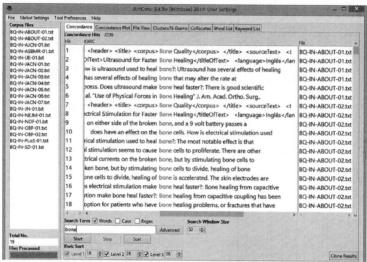

Figure 4.4: AntConc screenshot of concordance lines for *bone*.

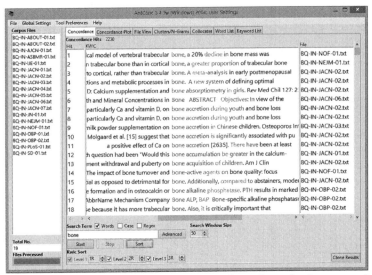

Figure 4.5: AntConc screenshot of concordance lines for *bone* sorted for 1st, 2nd and 3rd words to the right.

To make it easier for us to identify collocations, the lines can be sorted in different ways (**Kwic Sort** at the bottom of the screen). In the screenshot shown in Figure 4.5, the lines have been sorted by the first, then second, then third words to the right of *bone*.

We can clearly visualize the recurrence of *bone densitometry* and *bone density*. Another way of looking for usual combinations is searching for **Clusters**, the fourth tab at the top. This will give us all the two-word combinations with *bone*, but notice that they are not necessarily complete units of meaning, see Figure 4.6.

While *of bone* is not complete in itself, *bone mass* and *bone density* are perfect collocations as are many of the other ones shown in the screenshot. This is very helpful if you want to become familiar with the terminology of a certain specialized domain.

In the examples above we searched for a specific word, which we knew to be central in our domain, Bone Quality. But how do we find other words or expressions that we do not know about?

106

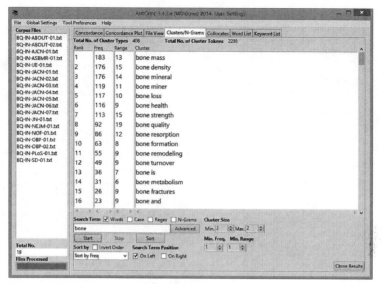

Figure 4.6: AntConc screenshot of clusters for *bone*.

Usually, the first step in searching a corpus is to generate a Word List, which will gives us ALL the words in our corpus. But first let us see how we load our corpus into AntConc. In the upper left-hand corner (Figure 4.7) there is a **File** tab which, when you click on it, will show a drop-down menu where you can either choose **Open File(s)** or **Open Dir**.

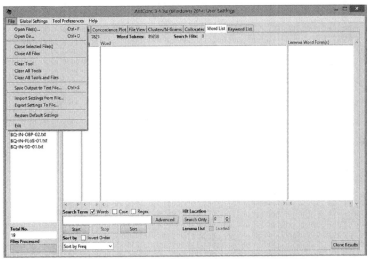

Figure 4.7: AntConc screenshot showing options under **File**.

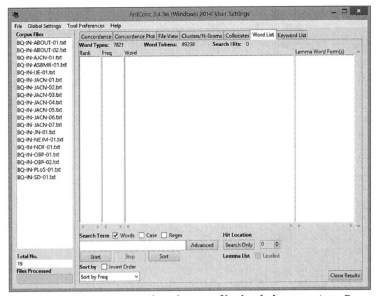

Figure 4.8: AntConc screenshot showing files loaded to constitute Bone Quality corpus.

Once this is done, all your files will be loaded and displayed, as shown in the screenshot shown in Figure 4.8.

We are now ready to generate a Word List by clicking on the sixth tab at the top of the screen. You can see what we get in Figure 4.9.

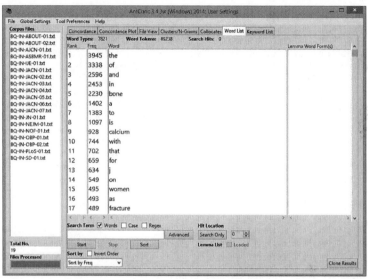

Figure 4.9: AntConc screenshot of Word List for Bone Quality corpus.

The screen shows the first 32 words in our corpus, but it also shows (in the top bar under the tabs) that **there are a total of 89,788 running words (tokens), out of which 9,064 are distinct words (types)**. For example, in the sentence *In our Bone Quality corpus bone is the most frequent noun* we have 11 tokens (running words), but only 10 types (distinct words, because *bone* occurs twice and is only counted once).

The most frequent words in any corpus are function words. These are words that act as the "glue" of sentences, such as *the, of, and*. They are also referred to as "closed-class words" or "stop words." In the example, the first content word, the noun *bone*, describes the topic of the corpus. In order to identify the words that are typical of our domain, we can search for Keywords. These are obtained by comparing our corpus with another larger corpus of a different domain, which can be a corpus of general language. Words with a statistically similar frequency will be canceled out leaving only the words that might be terms — or term candidates — in our corpus.

Notice that the function words have disappeared, and *bone* now heads the list of 1099 keywords in Figure 4.10. But you will also notice some initials. This is possibly due to faulty cleaning of the texts. In other words, these initials probably refer to the journals from which the texts were taken and may be part of the references. It is always a good idea either to eliminate the references or to set them between XML tags so that they will not be read by the system. This is not a major problem as long as you are aware of what the initials stand for. These can be seen (in Figure 4.11) when a concordance is generated.

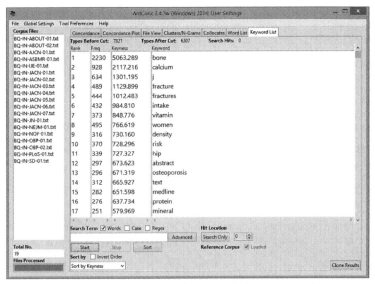

Figure 4.10: AntConc screenshot of Keywords for Bone Quality corpus.

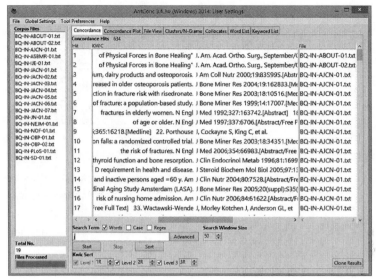

Figure 4.11: AntConc screenshot of concordance lines for *J*.

Once we have our Keyword list, we can search for different kinds of information. Let us look at a few examples. As *fracture(s)* is one of the most frequent words, you want to check if *spine fracture* is a possible collocation. If you generate a concordance for *fracture** you will get all words that begin with *fracture*. If you sort the concordance lines by the first word to the left, you will visualize all the words that precede these forms, and *spine fracture*, as expected, is one of them (Figure 4.12).

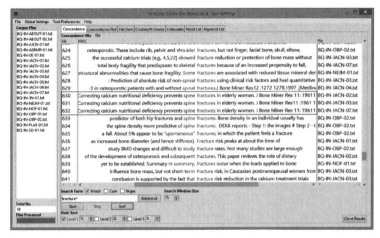

Figure 4.12: AntConc screenshot concordance lines for *fracture** sorted for 1st word to the left.

There are five occurrences of *spine fractures* and two of *spinal fractures*. Looking closer, though, you will notice that three of them (lines 630, 631, and 632) are the same and are actually the title of an article published in a journal. This reduces the number of occurrences to three, which seems to be a low number in a 90,000-word corpus. However, if we read the concordance lines down, we will see 45 occurrences of *vertebral fracture(s)*. This is exactly what Corpus Linguistics is able to show: although *spine fracture(s)* is a "possible" combination, the most "probable" way of referring to this type of fracture is *vertebral fracture(s)*. Being aware of this difference and using the most probable form — rather than just a grammatically possible form — will make your texts sound more natural and fluent.

Now let us suppose you do not know whether to say *supplementation in* or *supplementation on*. A corpus search for supplementation, sorting the concordance lines by the first word to the right might help. These are the results:

n a four-year clinical trial of Ca supplementation in adolescent girls [133]. There w
nteraction between activity and Ca supplementation in BMC (P = 0.05). There were sign
Iron status, menarche, and calcium supplementation in adolescent girls. Am J Clin Nut
f bone demineralization by calcium supplementation in precocious puberty during gonad
ons have responded more to calcium supplementation in most trials than trabecular-ric
indings on the benefits of calcium supplementation in prepubertal vs. pubertal childr
evention of bone loss by vitamin D supplementation in elderly women: a randomized dou
s PD, Vasey H, Bonjour JP: Dietary supplementation in elderly patients with fractured
s PD, Vasey H, Bonjour JP: Dietary supplementation in elderly patients with fractured
nsity [110,111]. The effect of Mg supplementation in humans is poorly understood bec
ical markers after one month of Mg supplementation in young women. In adolescent girl
, placebo-controlled trials of NaF supplementation in postmenopausal, osteoporotic wo
the effects of six months' protein supplementation in a group of elderly subjects pos
njour JP: Benefits of oral protein supplementation in elderly patients with fracture

. Effects of vitamin D and calcium supplementation on falls: a randomized controlled
led trial of the effect of calcium supplementation on bone density in postmenopausal
led trial of the effect of calcium supplementation on bone density in postmenopausal
up study of the effects of calcium supplementation on bone density in elderly postmen
e GD, Sharpe SJ: Effect of calcium supplementation on bone loss in postmenopausal wom
e SJ: Long-term effects of calcium supplementation on bone loss and fractures in post
ted a beneficial effect of calcium supplementation on the maintenance of bone mineral
ake modulates the effet of calcium supplementation on bone mass gain in prepubertal b
l of physical activity and calcium supplementation on bone mineral content in 3- to 5
ke modulates the effect of calcium supplementation on bone mineral mass gain in prepu
weather-Tait SJ: Effect of calcium supplementation on daily nonheme-iron absorption a
d LJ: Long-term effects of calcium supplementation on serum parathyroid hormone level
oral vitamin D3 (cholecalciferol) supplementation on fractures and mortality in men
E. Effect of calcium and vitamin D supplementation on bone density in men and women 6
cium, dairy product, and vitamin D supplementation on bone mass accrual and body comp
calcium or 25OH vitamin D3 dietary supplementation on bone loss at the hip in men and
W, Woo J: Benefits of milk powder supplementation on bone accretion in Chinese child
Villa LF, Rico H: Effects of zinc supplementation on vertebral and femoral bone mass

An examination of the context after the preposition will reveal that *in* usually precedes patients that will receive the supplementation, while *on* precedes some bone condition. Again, being aware of this difference will help you make your paper sound natural and fluent.

4.8 IN SUMMARY

In this chapter we have learned that language is made up of a great number of prefabricated chunks, which must be learned as a unit. You also became acquainted with various types of conventional language, mainly collocations and conventional expressions. You were introduced to Corpus Linguistics and learned how to search online corpora to clear language doubts you may have, but you also learned to build your own corpus and use stand-alone tools to query this corpus.

4.9 SUGGESTIONS FOR EXERCISES

You are now ready to do some exercises. Here are a few suggestions.

1. Find out which of the two forms below are more frequent in the COCA: (a) digitized — digitalized
   (b) comprehensive study — thorough study
   (c) present research — current research
2. Can *DO a study* and *MAKE a study* be used as synonyms? Look them up in the COCA to investigate how they are used.
3. Using only the Academic part of the COCA, investigate the word *work* preceded by a verb in 1-2 positions to the left. Does it occur more often as a verb or as a noun? When it occurs as a noun, what are the most frequent verbs used with it?
4. Using the Academic part of the COCA again, investigate which verbs usually precede and which verbs usually follow the word *data*.
5. Here is a suggestion for you to experience building your own corpus:
   (a) Build a small corpus with 5-10 texts in your area of study. Remember to save them in .txt format.
   (b) Make a Wordlist using AntConc.
   (c) Build a larger corpus (20-30 texts) with a variety of texts, preferably not academic.
   (d) Make a Keyword list with AntConc.
   (e) Using the AntConc Concordance, identify the most common collocations for the first word in your Keyword List.

Chapter 5

Sandra M. Aluísio
Valéria D. Feltrim

Writing Tools

In this chapter we introduce tools that support the writing of scientific papers. The first two sections describe three systems developed by our group, SciPo-Farmácia[9], Scien-Produção[10], and MAZEA-WEB[11] [23]. We then proceed to show SWAN[12], a text evaluation tool developed at the University of Eastern Finland [29].

SciPo-Farmácia is a Web-based system developed to assist non-native speakers of English, mainly Brazilians, with their scientific writing. The goal is to help you write a paper in a "top-down" approach, that is, starting from an outline and continuing down to paragraphs and sentences. This system was originally developed to help scientists in the pharmaceutical sciences, but its strategy and interface can be used by anyone who needs to write a scientific paper in English.

Scien-Producao has the same look-and-feel as SciPo-Farmacia but it also allows you to build your own text-base of papers to help with the writing of a paper in a specific domain.

MAZEA-WEB can automatically detect the rhetorical structure of an abstract. In other words, MAZEA-WEB identifies text segments that have a specific rhetorical role in a paper, such as "indicating the purpose" or "indicating a gap." This tool can help you improve your abstract by eliciting its components and helping you to identify missing expected components.

The last tool described is SWAN, a tool designed to help writers with content organization, without focusing on grammar or spelling. This tool guides you to proper scientific writing practices and helps you organize your paper.

---

[9] http://www.nilc.icmc.usp.br/scipo-farmacia/eng

[10] http://www.escritacientifica.sc.usp.br/scien-producao/

[11] "Multi-label Argumentative Zoning for English Abstracts" — http://www.nilc.icmc.usp.br/mazea-web/

[12] http://cs.joensuu.fi/swan

5.1 SciPo-Farmácia and Scien-Produção

5.1.1 SciPo-Farmácia

SciPo-Farmácia is a tool designed to assist non-native speakers of English with writing or drafting a scientific paper by guiding them through the overall structure of a paper and its sections.

SciPo-Farmácia is based on annotated sections of papers obtained from various publications related to the field of pharmaceutical sciences, such as *Nature, Science, Journal of Experimental Medicine (JEM), and The Journal of Biological Chemistry (JBC) Biotechnology Progress*. Its database is made up of 43 Abstracts, 39 Introductions, 30 Methods sections, 26 Results sections, 11 Discussions sections, and 22 Conclusions. The sections are of different lengths and sizes. They were analyzed for the quality of their writing and identified as matching the structure of current writing models. Although there is a predictable pattern in these papers, some of them combine the contents of multiple sections, such as conclusions and discussion, in a single section.

Let us observe how you can use SciPo-Farmácia to your advantage.

1. Access SciPo-Farmácia (http://www.nilc.icmc.usp.br/scipo-farmacia/eng/). On the home screen you can read about the tool's objectives, seek assistance (Help), and find author information (About SciPo-Farmácia) (see Fig. 5.1).

2. From the home screen, select one of the sections of papers: Abstracts, Introductions, Methods, Results, Discussions, and Conclusions. Let us assume for the current discussion that you have selected Abstracts (see Fig. 5.2).

3. Select the strategies and their order. In Fig. 5.3 we see the rhetorical structure of an abstract, its six components on the left, namely *Setting, Gap, Purpose, Methods and Materials, Main Results,* and *Conclusion,* and their associated strategies, totaling 22 for the abstract. To assist you in your selection, each item offers its own help link, explaining the component. In Fig. 5.3 we see the help window for the component, *Purpose* by clicking on the question mark (?).

You can select a specific strategy or a component. Selecting a component will retrieve abstracts with the given component, regardless of the strategy.

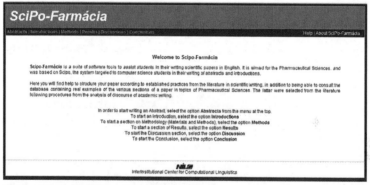

Figure 5.1: SciPo-Farmácia, home screen.

Figure 5.2: SciPo-Farmácia, home screen menu.

To write your own section of a paper, first select the desired strategies for each component, then choose the order in which you would like the components and their strategies to be organized in your text. The list of components and strategies is arranged in an order that has been found to be appropriate and clear for readers. We recommend that you follow that order to better structure your text.

If you do not understand what a specific strategy means or represents, you can browse through the sections and see examples, by clicking on "Case Base Navigation." In Fig. 5.4 we lists all 43 examples of abstracts in the database. In this screenshot, we have selected the fourth abstract (*ab*_4). We can also examine examples of strategies so that we can understand exactly what each one does before selecting it by clicking on "Sample of Strategies" (Fig. 5.4). You do not have to select all the strategies for each component, but your selection should remain consistent with what you want to report. If we select the component "Purpose," the "Specify the purpose" and "Introduce additional purposes" strategies will depend on the strategy "Indicate the main purpose." That means that either or both of the dependent strategies can be present with the strategy "Indicate the main purpose."

In the "Main Results" component, the "Comments about the results" strategy depends on the "Describe the results or Outline the results" strategy.

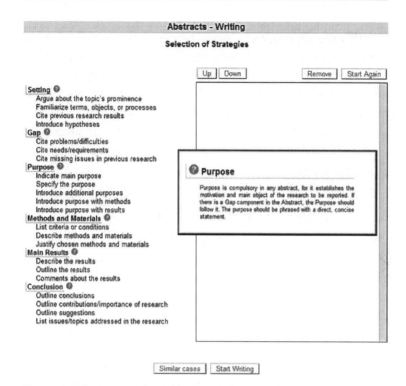

Figure 5.3: SciPo-Farmácia, Abstract screen.

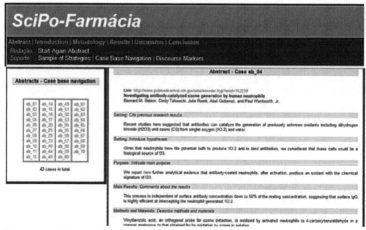

Figure 5.4: SciPo-Farmácia, a collection of 43 abstract examples.

This means that the "Comments about the results" strategy can only be used in addition to at least one other strategy of the "Results" component. The buttons let you modify your selection of components and strategies. The "Up" and "Down" buttons let you re-order the selected strategies. If you want to delete a strategy, select it and click "Remove." If you want to start over, click the "Start Again" button. If you wish to retrieve sections similar to the one you chose, click "Similar Cases" (Fig. 5.5).

4. Modify your selection or start writing. As soon as case examples appear, you can examine them, choose one, and start writing, or you can select additional strategies (see Fig. 5.6).
Double-click the selected case to open it; a window with the annotated text will appear (Fig. 5.7).

5. Edit the text. You can retrieve information about the number of words used in each component to meet the requirements of publications or conferences or you can examine other examples within the selected component (by clicking on "See Samples") or similar cases (by clicking on "Similar Cases") (Fig. 5.8).

You can include "reusable" (generic) parts of the examples in the section you are writing. In the example in Fig. 5.9 we show excerpts of setting, gap, and purpose being reused.

You can also select and modify discourse markers as the text is written by clicking on "Discourse markers" (Fig. 5.10).

Abstracts - Writing

Selection of Strategies

| Up | Down | | Remove | Start Again |

Setting
 Argue about the topic's prominence
 Familiarize terms, objects, or processes
 Cite previous research results
 Introduce hypotheses
Gap
 Cite problems/difficulties
 Cite needs/requirements
 Cite missing issues in previous research
Purpose
 Indicate main purpose
 Specify the purpose
 Introduce additional purposes
 Introduce purpose with methods
 Introduce purpose with results
Methods and Materials
 List criteria or conditions
 Describe methods and materials
 Justify chosen methods and materials
Main Results
 Describe the results
 Outline the results
 Comments about the results
Conclusion
 Outline conclusions
 Outline contributions/importance of research

Setting::Argue about the topic's prominence
Gap::Cite problems/difficulties
Purpose::Indicate main purpose

Figure 5.5: SciPo-Farmácia, showing the selection of 3 components for an abstract.

Abstracts - Recovered cases visualization

Chosen strategies:

Setting: *Argue about the topic's prominence*
Gap: *Cite problems/difficulties*
Purpose: *Indicate main purpose*

Change the selection of strategies

1. There are no cases with all the strategies chosen.

2. Cases with some of the strategies chosen:

ab_55 - 25.00%

3. There are no cases with all the strategies chosen, in different order than that previously chosen.

4. There are no cases with some of the chosen strategies in different order than that previously chosen.

Figure 5.6: SciPo-Farmácia showing a case recovered in which 25 percent match the request ("Chosen strategies").

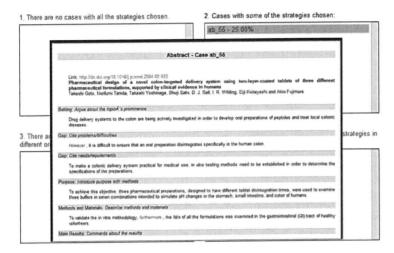

Figure 5.7: SciPo-Farmácia, showing the recovered abstract.

| Similar Cases | Change Strategies |

Setting ⊘
Argue about the topic's prominence   See Samples

Characters / Words :   0 / 0

Gap ⊘
Cite problems/difficulties   See Samples

Characters / Words :   0 / 0

Purpose ⊘
Indicate main purpose   See Samples

Characters / Words :   0 / 0

| Join components in a file |

Figure 5.8: SciPo-Farmácia, Text composition window.

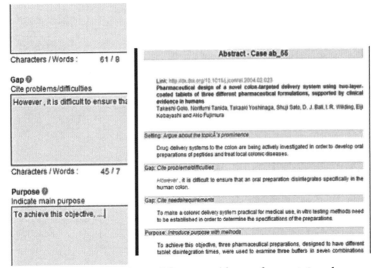

Figure 5.9: SciPo-Farmácia, adding reusable text from retrieved cases.

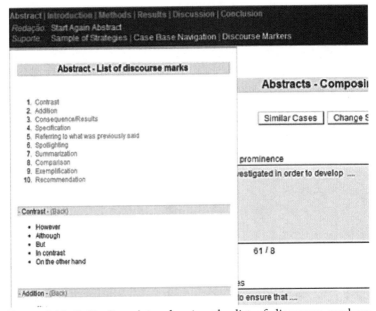

Figure 5.10: SciPo-Farmácia, showing the list of discourse markers commonly used in abstracts.

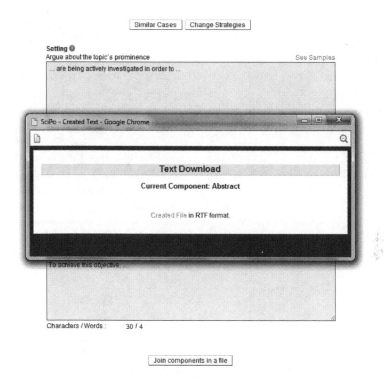

Figure 5.11: SciPo-Farmácia, saving the edited text in RTF format.

6. Save the generated file in the RTF format. This is the final step. The saved text can then be edited using any word processor (Fig. 5.11).

5.1.2 SCIEN-PRODUÇÃO

Scien-Produção (Scientific English Produção, which is Portuguese for Scientific English Production) is a writing tool to assist students and Production Engineering researchers in their writing in English. It was created by integrating an adapted version of Scipo-Farmácia, shown in Fig. 5.12, with *BRAT* [13]

---

[13] http://brat.nlplab.org/

(BratRapidAnnotation Tool), illustrated in Fig. 5.13. Scien-Produção helps the user read and annotate scientific papers, in order to create his/her own corpus of text-base of annotated papers. This corpus will be then used for the learning-by-example strategy.

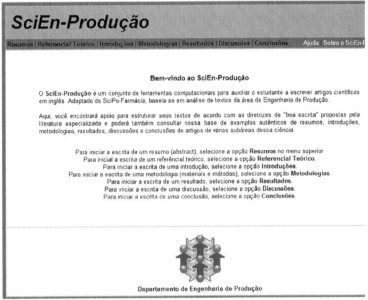

Figure 5.12: Home screen of Scien-Produção (in Portuguese).

BRAT is a freely available, web-based tool that can be customized to assist in annotating scientific articles. It encompasses three steps: reading, identification of writing strategies, and annotation. It thus facilitates annotation not only for beginners but also for experienced users. This should increase productivity, reduce costs, and save human effort.

Although built with Production Engineering papers in mind, Scien-Producao is based on a dynamic case base, which can be easily adapted to other areas of science and technology.

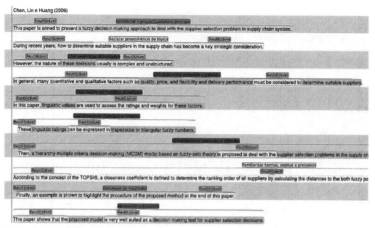

Figure 5.13: Abstract annotated with the help of BRAT.

5.2 MAZEA-WEB

MAZEA-WEB 2.0 is a tool for identifying sections and/or components of a given abstract. It identifies six components: Background, Gap, Purpose, Methods, Results, and Conclusion. MAZEA-WEB uses machine-learning techniques to identify the sections. It accepts a plain-text abstract as input, and it outputs the abstract with the identified sections marked. This can help you as you revise your abstract; you can add or change sections or rewrite the abstract.

Using MAZEA-WEB is relatively simple. First, enter the text of an abstract, and select the category to which the abstract belongs (of the following eight):

- Life and Health Sciences
- Physical Sciences and Engineering
- Electric, Mechanical, and Industrial Engineering
- Physics
- Dentistry

- Biology, Biophysics, and Bioengineering
- Pharmaceutical Sciences
- Computer Science

Then click "Detect Rhetorical Structure" to run the program. Let us go step by step.

Let us use the following abstract from Amancio [30]:

Methods from statistical physics, such as those involving complex networks, have been increasingly used in quantitative analysis of linguistic phenomena. In this paper, we represented pieces of text with different levels of simplification in cooccurrence networks and found that topological regularity correlated negatively with textual complexity. Furthermore, in less complex texts the distance between concepts, represented as nodes, tended to decrease. The complex networks metrics were treated with multivariate pattern recognition techniques, which allowed us to distinguish between original texts and their simplified versions. For each original text, two simplified versions were generated manually with increasing number of simplification operations. As expected, distinction was easier for the strongly simplified versions, where the most relevant metrics were node strength, shortest paths and diversity. Also, the discrimination of complex texts was improved with higher hierarchical network metrics, thus pointing to the usefulness of considering wider contexts around the concepts. Though the accuracy rate in the distinction was not as high as in methods using deep linguistic knowledge, the complex network approach is still useful for a rapid screening of texts whenever assessing complexity is essential to guarantee accessibility to readers with limited reading ability.

MAZEA 2.0

MAZEA (Multi-label Argumentative Zoning for English Abstracts) is a machine learning classifier which automatically identifies rhetorical moves in English abstracts, enabling a given sentence to be assigned to as many categories as appropriate. The categories considered are: (i) **background**, (ii) **gap**, (iii) **purpose**, (iv) **method**, (v) **result**, and (vi) **conclusion**.

In its initial version, MAZEA focused on two broad fields: **physical sciences and engineering (PE) and life and health sciences (LH)**. MAZEA has been successfully used in English academic writing courses as a pedagogical resource tool. Learners are first asked to write an abstract for their research projects and then identify the moves they have used and how they were organized. These abstracts are then submitted to MAZEA and learners can compare their categorization with the system's. The idea is to have students reflecting on the move structure of their own abstracts and raise their awareness of key aspects related to text organization.

MAZEA 2.0 is a version adapted to different disciplines with different conventions and ways of expressing their ideas and arguments. This version processes abstracts based on six group of disciplines: Engineering (**electrical engineering, industrial engineering, mechanical engineering**), **Biology** (biology, bioengineering, biophysics), **Computer Science, Pharmaceutical Sciences, Physics** and **Dentistry**.

The eight corpora used to train MAZEA and MAZEA 2.0 are made publicly available in this website (click on "Downloads" below).

Before using:
1. Files must be in the txt format (encoded in UTF-8)
2. Max size: 5 MB

⊛ Enter your text:

```
Methods from statistical physics, such as those involving complex networks, have been
increasingly used in quantitative analysis of linguistic phenomena. In this paper, we
represented pieces of text with different levels of simplification in co-occurrence
networks and found that topological regularity correlated negatively with textual
complexity. Furthermore, in less complex texts the distance between concepts,
represented as nodes, tended to decrease. The complex networks metrics were treated
with multivariate pattern recognition techniques, which allowed us to distinguish
between original texts and their simplified versions. For each original text, two
simplified versions were generated manually with increasing number of simplification
operations. As expected, distinction was easier for the strongly simplified versions,
where the most relevant metrics were node strength, shortest paths and diversity.
Also the discrimination of complex texts was improved with higher hierarchical
```

Figure 5.14: Running MAZEA-WEB with an abstract from the "Physical Sciences and Engineering" field.

In Figure 5.14 we show the initial screen of MAZEA-WEB, with the text above as input. We have selected Physical Sciences and Engineering as the category of the abstract. Now let us click "Detect Rhetoric Structure" to run MAZEA-WEB.

The output shows the abstract's text annotated to identify each component.

This enables you to verify that the structure of your abstract is adequate. It can also help you determine whether or not any required sections are missing.

Your results may differ depending on the choice you have selected. The eight available options differ in terms of the corpus that was used in training MAZEA-WEB. In our example, the tool generated better results when we selected "Physical Sciences and Engineering" (Fig. 5.15) than "Computer Science" (Fig. 5.16), although it made several mistakes in classifying the abstract.

Background
Methods from statistical physics, such as those involving complex networks, have been increasingly used in quantitative analysis of linguistic phenomena.

Purpose
In this paper, we represented pieces of text with different levels of simplification in co-occurrence networks and found that topological regularity correlated negatively with textual complexity.

Method
Furthermore, in less complex texts the distance between concepts, represented as nodes, tended to decrease.

Method
The complex networks metrics were treated with multivariate pattern recognition techniques, which allowed us to distinguish between original texts and their simplified versions.

Result
For each original text, two simplified versions were generated manually with increasing number of simplification operations.

Gap
As expected, distinction was easier for the strongly simplified versions, where the most relevant metrics were node strength, shortest paths and diversity.

Method
Also, the discrimination of complex texts was improved with higher hierarchical network metrics, thus pointing to the usefulness of considering wider contexts around the concepts.

Method
Though the accuracy rate in the distinction was not as high as in methods using deep linguistic knowledge, the complex network approach is still useful for a rapid screening of texts whenever assessing complexity is essential to guarantee accessibility to readers with limited reading ability.

Figure 5.15: Running MAZEA-WEB, result of analyzing a computer science abstract using a classifier trained with a "Physical Sciences and Engineering" corpus.

Background
Methods from statistical physics, such as those involving complex networks, have been increasingly used in quantitative analysis of linguistic phenomena.

Purpose
In this paper, we represented pieces of text with different levels of simplification in co-occurrence networks and found that topological regularity correlated negatively with textual complexity.

Method
Furthermore, in less complex texts the distance between concepts, represented as nodes, tended to decrease.

Method
The complex networks metrics were treated with multivariate pattern recognition techniques, which allowed us to distinguish between original texts and their simplified versions.

Method
For each original text, two simplified versions were generated manually with increasing number of simplification operations.

Method
As expected, distinction was easier for the strongly simplified versions, where the most relevant metrics were node strength, shortest paths and diversity.

Method
Also, the discrimination of complex texts was improved with higher hierarchical network metrics, thus pointing to the usefulness of considering wider contexts around the concepts.

Method
Though the accuracy rate in the distinction was not as high as in methods using deep linguistic knowledge, the complex network approach is still useful for a rapid screening of texts whenever assessing complexity is essential to guarantee accessibility to readers with limited reading ability.

Figure 5.16: Running MAZEA-WEB, result of analyzing a computer science abstract using a classifier trained with a "Computer Science" corpus.

When the abstract was classified within the "Physical Sciences and Engineering" as shown in Fig. 5.15, MAZEA identified five components:

1. Background,
2. Gap,
3. Purpose,
4. Methods, and
5. Results.

It failed to identify the Conclusion component and did not preserve the order that is traditionally proposed for scientific papers with regards to the Gap: it was listed after the Results components, followed by additional Methods component.

When the abstract was classified within the "Computer Science" category, see Fig. 5.16, MAZEA-WEB identified three components:

1. Background,
2. Purpose, and
3. Methods.

It failed to identify the remaining three components:

1. Gap,
2. Results, and
3. Conclusion.

An interesting way to illustrate the behavior of MAZEA-WEB is to compare its output with one that has been manually annotated by the authors. To do so, we will use the example shown in Chapter 2, where the authors specified the sections. In Fig. 5.17 below we show the abstract as it has been annotated by the authors. It includes four sections: Purpose, Methods, Results, and Conclusion.

Next, we remove the section labels from the abstract in order to obtain only its text. We use this text as input to MAZEA-WEB and select "Life and Health Sciences." We selected this classification because of the topic and area discussed in the abstract (see Fig. 5.18).

⊞ Validity of the computer science and applications (CSA) activity monitor in children.
(PMID:9565947)

| Abstract | Citations ◎ | BioEntities ◎ | Related Articles ◎ |

Trost SG, Ward DS, Moorehead SM, Watson PD, Riner W, Burke JR
Department of Exercise Science, University of South Carolina, Columbia, USA.
Medicine and Science in Sports and Exercise [1998, 30(4):629-633]

Type: Journal Article
DOI: 10.1097/00005768-199804000-00023 ◎

Abstract

Highlight Terms ◎
☐ Chemicals(1)

PURPOSE: The purpose of this study was to evaluate the validity of the CSA activity monitor as a measure of children's physical activity using energy expenditure (EE) as a criterion measure.

METHODS: Thirty subjects aged 10 to 14 performed three 5-min treadmill bouts at 3, 4, and 6 mph, respectively. While on the treadmill, subjects wore CSA (WAM 7164) activity monitors on the right and left hips. VO2 was monitored continuously by an automated system. EE was determined by multiplying the average VO2 by the caloric equivalent of the mean respiratory exchange ratio.

RESULTS: Repeated measures ANOVA indicated that both CSA monitors were sensitive to changes in treadmill speed. Mean activity counts from each CSA unit were not significantly different and the intraclass reliability coefficient for the two CSA units across all speeds was 0.87. Activity counts from both CSA units were strongly correlated with EE (r = 0.86 and 0.87, P < 0.001). An EE prediction equation was developed from 20 randomly selected subjects and cross-validated on the remaining 10. The equation predicted mean EE within 0.01 kcal.min-1. The correlation between actual and predicted values was 0.93 (P < 0.01) and the SEE was 0.93 kcal.min-1.

CONCLUSION: These data indicate that the CSA monitor is a valid and reliable tool for quantifying treadmill walking and running in children.

Figure 5.17: Manually annotated abstract.

Before using:
1. Files must be in the txt format (encoded in UTF-8)
2. Max size: 5 MB

◉ Enter your text:

The purpose of this study was to evaluate the validity of the CSA activity monitor as a measure of children's physical activity using energy expenditure (EE) as a criterion measure. Thirty subjects aged 10 to 14 performed three 5-min treadmill bouts at 3, 4, and 6 mph, respectively. While on the treadmill, subjects wore CSA (WAM 7164) activity monitors on the right and left hips. VO2 was monitored continuously by an automated system. EE was determined by multiplying the average VO2 by the caloric equivalent of the mean respiratory exchange ratio. Repeated measures ANOVA indicated that both CSA monitors were sensitive to changes in treadmill speed. Mean activity counts from each CSA unit were not significantly different and the intraclass reliability coefficient for the two CSA units across all speeds was 0.87. Activity counts from both CSA units were strongly correlated with EE (r = 0.86 and 0.87, P < 0.001). An EE prediction equation was developed from 20 randomly selected subjects and cross-validated on the remaining 10. The equation predicted mean EE within 0.01 kcal.min-1. The correlation between actual and predicted values was 0.93 (P < 0.01) and the SEE was 0.93 kcal.min-1. These data indicate that the CSA monitor is a valid and reliable tool for quantifying treadmill walking and running in children.

○ Upload Abstract: (Choose File) No file chosen

Figure 5.18: The abstract's text without labels, entered as input to MAZEA-WEB and using the Life and Health Sciences classification

In Fig. 5.19 we show the output generated by MAZEA-WEB. Let us compare the original, manual annotation with the one generated by MAZEA-WEB:

1. **Purpose:** both annotations show the same text labeled as Purpose
2. **Methods:** the original methods identified by the authors match part of MAZEA-WEB's output. MAZEA-WEB annotated one additional sentence as Methods
3. **Results:** The first sentence in the original abstract annotated as Results was instead annotated as Methods by MAZEA-WEB. The span of the results matches both annotations. However, MAZEA-WEB introduced a sentence in between labeled as Methods.
4. **Conclusion:** Both annotations, manual and automatic (MAZEA-WEB), match in their label and segmentation of the text.

What can we learn from this exercise? First, annotations will vary significantly, even with all the possible training. Second, comparing a manual annotation with an automatic one generated by MAZEA-WEB, as in this example, will force you to rethink how to structure and organize the sections in the abstract. This may entail rewriting sections or parts of the abstract, reorganizing sections, or starting all over.

www.nilc.icmc.usp.br/mazea-web/results.php

Purpose
The purpose of this study was to evaluate the validity of the CSA activity monitor as a measure of children's physica

Method
Thirty subjects aged 10 to 14 performed three 5-min treadmill bouts at 3, 4, and 6 mph, respectively.

Method
While on the treadmill, subjects wore CSA (WAM 7164) activity monitors on the right and left hips.

Method
VO2 was monitored continuously by an automated system.

Method
EE was determined by multiplying the average VO2 by the caloric equivalent of the mean respiratory exchange rati

Method
Repeated measures ANOVA indicated that both CSA monitors were sensitive to changes in treadmill speed.

Result
Mean activity counts from each CSA unit were not significantly different and the intraclass reliability coefficient for

Result
Activity counts from both CSA units were strongly correlated with EE (r = 0.86 and 0.87, P < 0.001).

Method
An EE prediction equation was developed from 20 randomly selected subjects and cross-validated on the remaining

Result
The equation predicted mean EE within 0.01 kcal.min-1.

Result
The correlation between actual and predicted values was 0.93 (P < 0.01) and the SEE was 0.93 kcal.min-1.

Conclusion
These data indicate that the CSA monitor is a valid and reliable tool for quantifying treadmill walking and running i

Figure 5.19: Output generated by MAZEA-WEB with Life and Health Sciences classification.

5.3 SWAN

SWAN[14] *(Scientific Writing AssistaNt)* is a tool for evaluating an already written article. While tools like SciPo-Farmácia help you plan and write the first draft of your paper, SWAN helps you review what you have already written. The focus, however, is not on possible spelling and grammatical errors, but on the organization of content and the fluidity of each section. The goal is to help you write clearer and to make your writing easier to understand, or more reader-friendly. Unlike SciPo-Farmácia, SWAN was not

---

[14] Available at http://cs.joensuu.fi/swan

designed to assist non-natives, in that no resources of this tool address English language problems. Still, SWAN can help you assess whether the organization of the content is appropriate as well as identify other issues that often go unnoticed, such as very long sentences and excessive use of the passive voice.

To demonstrate how SWAN can assist you, we provide examples of some evaluations and how to obtain them using the tool. A complete demonstration of all of SWAN's features is beyond the scope of this book. See the official site for code download, startup, and installation instructions, tutorials, and the user manual.

As stated earlier, SWAN evaluates a text that has already been written. Before starting to use it you will need the file of your paper to be open and ready to use. You will provide SWAN with your text by copying each section of the paper and pasting it in the corresponding spot. Thus, it is important that the file be in a format that is compatible with clean copying. Plain text files as well other document formats are compatible. Text from PDF files may require additional editing since the format of the pasted text may differ from that of the original text.

When you first launch SWAN, you will see the main menu (see Fig. 5.20). Here you can choose one of two evaluation options: (1) automatic, and (2) manual. Automatic evaluation focuses on content organization. In this mode, you get evaluations of the paper's title and its sections and subsections as well as the rhetorical structures and fluidity of the text of the Abstract, Introduction, and Conclusion. Manual evaluation focuses on the analysis of textual fluidity; it can be applied to any section. "Fluidity" within SWAN means that the text is "easy to understand." This translates into the connection between the sentences. A sentence is "fluid" if it connects well to the preceding and following sentences.

In Fig. 5.20 we show how you can choose between two automatic evaluation options: "Quick Start" or "Full Evaluation."

You can also choose to recover data used in a previous session ("Load previous SWAN session"). The arrows point to text boxes under each option that explain the circumstances for choosing one over another.

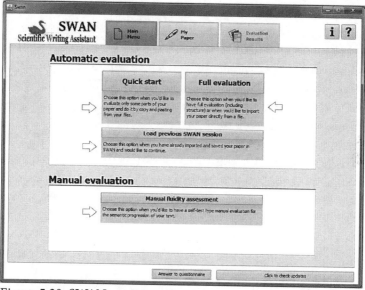

Figure 5.20: SWAN, main menu.

Selecting "Quick Start," you can insert your text in the tool, as shown in Fig. 5.21. The vertical arrow points to the tabs that allow you to choose which section of the article to be evaluated. In this figure we selected the title. For the tool to evaluate the title, you need to fill out several information items in addition to the input text.

In Fig. 5.21, arrow (1) shows the text box where you will paste the title of the paper. Once the title has been inserted, all the words of the title are transferred to the second text box, indicated by arrow (2). There you can join two or more words to form a single keyword (or keyphrase), if desired, as we have done with "Rhetorical Moves" and "Multi-label Classifiers Sentence." To join words, just select them and click the "Join" button. You must also select the keywords in your title that are directly related to the contribution of the research, as we have done with the keywords "Rhetorical Moves," "Multi-label Classifiers Sentence," and "Annotated Corpora." You should also check if the keywords of the title are good search keys and classify them according to the level of knowledge required to use them: generic search, search expert, intermediate search, none of those. The third text box, indicated by arrow (3), asks you to select portions of your title and associate them with the rhetorical functions shown. In this example, we have associated the phrase "Rhetorical Move Detection" with the "Main application of your research," and the phrase "Multi-label Classifiers Sentence" was associated with the "Used methodology to determine the results of your research" . When done, choose "Start Evaluation" (button with the arrow).

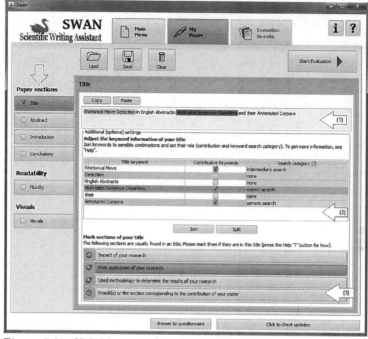

Figure 5.21: SWAN screenshot: Title

The result of our evaluation is shown in Fig. 5.22. The tool found that our title is clear, but drew our attention to other aspects that may be problematic. For example, no "attractive" words, such as adjectives and adverbs, were found, and several contributive keywords have been spread throughout the title. Now you can return to the previous screen (Fig. 5.20) by clicking the "My Paper" tab, modify your title according to the suggestions given, and obtain a new assessment ("Start evaluation"). In this example, we are pleased with our title, so we will move on to review the abstract. To do this, click the "Abstract" tab (left in Fig. 5.20 – Paper sections)

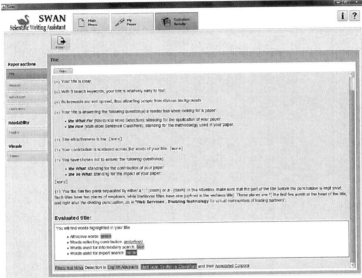

Figure 5.22: SWAN screenshot: Results of the evaluation of the title.

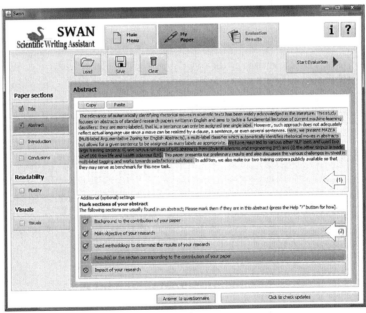

Figure 5.23: SWAN screenshot: Abstract.

Similar to the case of title analysis, certain details need to be provided in order to evaluate the abstract. Let us see how this can be done (Fig. 5.23).

In Fig. 5.23, arrow (1) points to the first text box. Paste your abstract here. In the second box (arrow (2)), select sentences of your abstract and match each one of them to one of the listed rhetorical functions. In our example, the sentence "The relevance of automatically identifying rhetorical moves in scientific texts has been widely acknowledged in the literature" was marked as "Background". Similarly for sentences that were labeled as "Main Objective", "Methodology", and "Results". No sentence was marked as "Impact of your research." When everything has been filled out, click "Start Evaluation".

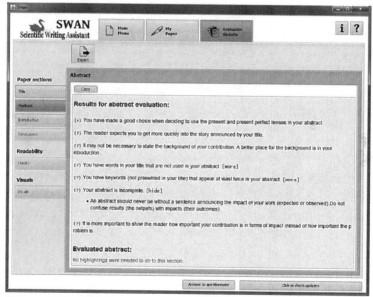

Figure 5.24: SWAN screenshot: Results of the evaluation of the abstract.

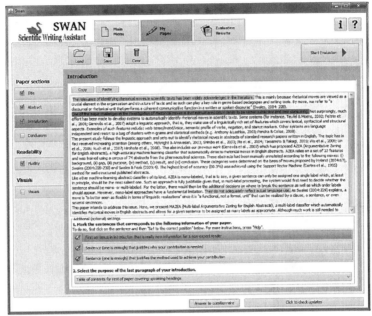

Figure 5.25: SWAN screenshot: Introduction.

The result of our abstract example is shown in Fig. 5.24. The tool considered it a good idea to use the present tense. With respect to the rhetorical structure, the tool suggests that sentences with the "Background" function should not be in the abstract. It also draws our attention to the fact that no sentence in the abstract emphasizes the impact of the research. The tool further explains that it is more important to show the reader the importance of the paper's contribution in terms of its impact than in terms of its relevance to the problem addressed. In addition to the comments about the structure, the evaluation also points out that there are keywords in the title that do not appear in the abstract and vice versa. Again, you can return to the screen shown in Fig. 5.20 by clicking the "My Paper" tab, modify the abstract according to the suggestions given, and obtain a new evaluation ("Start Evaluation").

For the introduction, the procedure is similar to the one for the abstract. However, instead of asking for a finer rhetorical structure, as was done in the abstract, the tool only requests some information, such as justification of the work (both its contribution and the methodology used), as shown in Fig. 5.25.

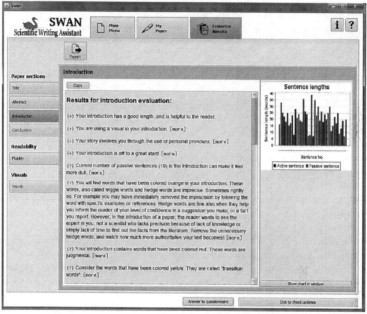

Figure 5.26: SWAN screenshot: Results of the evaluation of the introduction.

The evaluation result of our example introduction is shown in Fig. 5.26. The evaluation of the introduction is less focused on structure and more on issues such as the use of the passive voice, the use of pronouns, and the length of sentences. Notice the graph that shows the sizes and voice (active/passive) of the sentences of your introduction on the right-hand side of Fig. 5.26. This will help you avoid having very long sentences and using the passive voice. Here it is important to remember that while the passive voice is used extensively in scientific texts written in Portuguese, in English it is preferable to use the active voice. As a matter of fact, many prominent publications have recently released new instructions for authors in which they explicitly emphasize, in no ambiguous terms, that authors must write in the active voice as much as possible. This implies that papers written extensively in the passive voice will not be accepted.

Other comments about the introduction include the use of hedge words (e.g., widely), judgmental words (e.g., worst), and transition words (e.g., in addition).

The evaluation of the conclusion section is simpler. All you have to do is select the "Conclusion" tab on the left side of the screen, paste the text of the conclusion in the text box, and run the evaluation. Our conclusion example is shown in Fig. 5.27, and the result of the evaluation is shown in Fig. 5.28.

As can be seen in Fig. 5.28, the conclusion evaluation does not point to any structural issues. In this example, the tool found it positive that the conclusion was longer than the abstract, but questioned the use of the present tense. This is because SWAN expects most conclusion verbs to be in the past tense.

When you select "Full evaluation" rather than "Quick start," SWAN also evaluates the paper's structure in terms of the distribution of text among the various sections and subsections and their titles. Information about the titles must be entered manually. You will also need to identify the sections that refer to the contribution of your paper. To illustrate this analysis, we show the structure of an example paper in Fig. 5.29 and the evaluation result in Fig. 5.30.

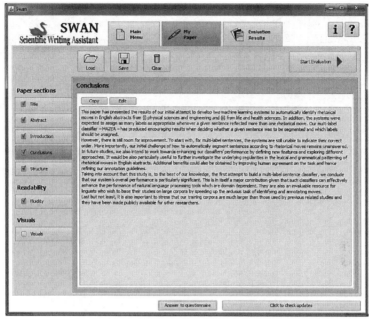

Figure 5.27: SWAN screenshot: Conclusion.

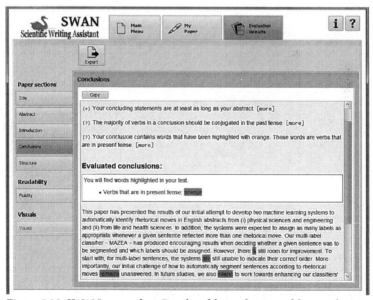

Figure 5.28: SWAN screenshot: Results of the evaluation of the conclusion.

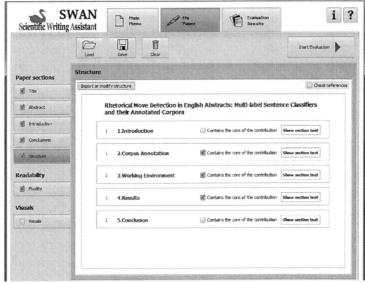

Figure 5.29: SWAN screenshot: Structure.

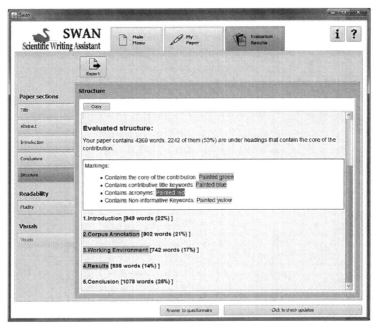

Figure 5.30: SWAN screenshot: Results of the evaluation of the structure

5.4 IN SUMMARY

In this chapter we have learned how to use SciPo-Farmácia and MAZEA-WEB to help us write a better paper and how to use SWAN to analyze and improve an already-written text.

SciPo-Farmácia and Scien-Produção will assist you in planning your paper structure and writing a first draft; MAZEA-WEB will help you structure and revise your abstract; and SWAN will help you evaluate your writing, by checking various aspects of your paper.

CHAPTER 6

Carmen Dayrell

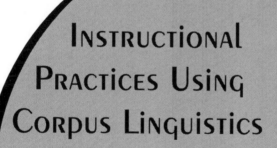

INSTRUCTIONAL PRACTICES USING CORPUS LINGUISTICS

This chapter discusses textual patterns identified in research papers. We first introduce the concept of patterns and explain the significant role they play in scientific writing. Then, we discuss how these patterns can be identified. We do this by examining key aspects of the various sections of a standard research paper.

6.1 TEXTUAL PATTERNS

Textual patterns are recurrent combinations of words that are typically used in a given genre. Examples of textual patterns in research papers are: **as a result of, the present study proposes, it is argued that, the results show that, we find that, this paper concludes with,** and so on. Here, it is important to stress that such chunks of words are not necessarily fixed, that is, there may be variations within them. In general, variations refer to:

1. Different forms of a given verb, such as the verb TO BE in the following examples:
    - it **is** argued that
    - it **was** argued that
    - it **has been** argued that

2. Different lexical choices. For instance, in the following examples, a number of verbs can fill the blank in *the results * that* :
    - the results **show** that
    - the results **indicate** that
    - the results **suggest** that

3. Some words, or sequences of words, that may be inserted within the pattern or in its surrounding

context. This is the case of all words in bold in the examples below:

- We **also** found that
- The results **clearly** demonstrate that
- This paper **briefly** describes
- The findings **reported here** indicate that
- **In this study**, we have argued that
- **Here**, it is suggested that

It is also important to mention that there may be multiple variations within patterns. Let us examine the examples below:

1	The	aim	of	this	study	is	to	develop
2	The	purpose	of	this	study	was	to	describe
3	The	purpose	of	the present	paper	is	to	report
4	The	goal	of	this	research	is	to	compare
5	The	objective	of	the current	article	is	to	discuss

We notice that "aim" (example 1) can be replaced with several semantically related words such as *purpose*, *goal*, and *objective*, shown in examples 2 to 5. In the slot where *this* appears, we may use "*the present*" or "*the current*." *Study* may be replaced with words such as *paper*, *research*, or *article*. The verb TO BE may be used in its present (is) and past (was) tenses. Various verbs that describe a purpose (e.g., develop, describe, report, compare, and discuss) may be used after to.

6.1.1 WHY ARE TEXTUAL PATTERNS OF SPECIAL INTEREST?

Novice writers can benefit from learning about textual patterns because their recurrent use is said to be closely associated with fluent linguistic production. As Ken Hyland ([31], [32]) explains, competent speakers of a language can distinguish what is usual and natural in a particular context from what is only grammatical. This means that competent speakers are aware of the textual patterns used by their discourse community and hence make use of them on a regular basis.

The recurrent use of familiar textual patterns is said to facilitate communication by making language more predictable to the listener or reader and reducing processing time [31, 32, 33]. By contrast, the absence of such patterns may be an indication of lack of fluency of a new speaker of a language [31, 32]. Thus, gaining control of a new genre requires "*a sensitivity to expert users' preferences for certain sequences of words over others which might be equally possible*" [34, p. 236].

6.1.2 DO NOVICE AND EXPERT WRITERS USE SIMILAR PATTERNS?

A number of scholars have shown that the language produced by students and novice writers is different from that of experts, irrespective of whether novices are native or non-native speakers of English. As Milton and Hyland [35, p. 149] put it, "*There is a huge gulf between NS [native speaker] student papers and the professionally edited articles of experience academics, and ... it takes years of professional apprenticeship before NSs adopt the norms of their academic discourse community.*" This is mainly because inexperienced writers are not always aware of the conventions of academic discourse, whether in terms of text organization or linguistic choices (lexical features and syntactical constructions).

For those writing in a foreign language, there are even more daunting challenges. In addition to mastering the lexical and syntactical features of the target language, non-native speakers should be aware that practices, expectations, and values may vary across languages. This means that transferring the conventions and practices of your mother tongue to the target language may fail, even when you produce a text that is grammatically correct. To use language effectively, one needs to quickly learn how to use language in the way that is expected by the respective disciplinary community.

Another important point to stress here is that, as a rule, the vocabulary of second and foreign-language learners tends to be more limited than that of native speakers of the language in question. Thus, learners of a foreign language tend to draw more heavily on the words and expressions with which they are familiar and, as a result, overuse some items while underusing others. For example, Dayrell [36, 37] finds relevant differences related to lexical choices when comparing abstracts of research papers written in English by Brazilian graduate students of physics, pharmaceutical sciences, and computer science with those published by leading international journals in the same disciplines. The verbs USE, PRESENT, and OBTAIN had a significantly higher frequency in students' abstracts: 84.9, 27.6, and 20.1 instances per 10,000 words respectively in comparison with 52.5, 17.0, and 11.9 in published abstracts. Although these verbs were used properly, these higher frequencies in students' abstracts show that novice writers tend to be repetitive in their lexical choices. They may do so because they lack the knowledge about words or terms that can be used instead. Since academic writing is expected to present reasonable lexical variation, such tendency to repeat words or phrases requires special attention. Dayrell's analyses also revealed that some verbs tend to be underused by students. For instance, FIND occurs 11.7 times per 10,000 words in students' abstracts and 17.1 in published abstracts.

6.1.3 IDENTIFYING TEXTUAL PATTERNS

In what follows, we focus on the identification of textual patterns within different sections of a research paper. For each section, we first look at examples of patterns. You will then be asked to examine the papers from **your own corpus** (see Chapter 3, Section 3.2.2). This is, in fact, a key task in our discussion as it enables you to identify the patterns typically used by **your** academic community. Although certain features are commonly recognized as widespread in research writing, disciplines may vary considerably in terms of their preferred patterns [38, p. 3].

Once we identify those patterns, we look for potential variations within them. For some patterns, we will explore variations by turning to the *Corpus of Contemporary American English* (COCA — http://www.americancorpus.org; see Chapter 4).

When using COCA, you may be asked to specify the grammatical category of your search word. For convenience, here are the notations for the grammatical categories that are frequently used:

$[nn*] \Rightarrow$ noun $[v*] \Rightarrow$ verb $[j*] \Rightarrow$ adjective
$[r*] \Rightarrow$ adverb $[i*] \Rightarrow$ preposition $[c*] \Rightarrow$ conjunction

6.2 ABSTRACTS

Abstracts are viewed as the gatekeepers for scientific papers. Deciding whether or not to read a full paper usually depends on the reader's impression and understanding of the abstract. A carefully tailored abstract can only help to enhance a reviewer's impression of the paper [39, p. 2].

In Chapters 2 and 3, we discussed how abstracts are usually structured and presented their most typical components: background, gap, purpose, method, results, and conclusion. Here, we focus on the linguistic choices within the purpose and result components. We will address the other components of abstracts afterward when we discuss the remaining sections of a paper.

6.2.1 ABSTRACTS: STATING THE PURPOSE OF THE STUDY

Research papers are expected to state the purpose of the research. The purpose responds to the "why" of the research. In this section, we explore ways of stating the purposes of the study described in a paper. We first identify textual patterns that are commonly used to this end and then look at typical "purposive" verbs. These are some verbs that express the action to be carried out: *propose, present, develop,* and so on.

Below are examples of textual patterns (marked in **bold**) frequently used in the *purpose* component of abstracts. Examine the examples within each group. Can you identify common features among them?

1. • **We introduce** previewing tools to facilitate the process ...
   • **In this paper we investigate** the notion of ...
   • Using a statistical calculation, **we explore** the properties of ...

2. • **This paper describes** a project to perform ...
   • **This study examines** the record of various flow phases in ...
   • **This article addresses** Internet search problems by considering ...

3. • **The purpose of this study is to understand** the behavior and ...
   • **The objective of this study was to determine** the effects of the ...
   • **The aim of the paper is to provide** an integrated method ...

4. • **The goal is to find** the same fine-scale mixing in the ...
   • **The purpose** here **is to explore** some abstractions that help read ...

- **Our aim was to determine** the mechanism of ...

5.
- A suite of ... methods ... was used **to examine** the mineralogy of ...
- ... spectroscopy was used **to study** the linewidth and ...
- **To investigate** the trade-offs between ... we compare ...

6.
- Low-and high-field magnetotransport measurements ... **are reported**.
- Models for compensation of measurement overhead in par **are described**.
- ... mtdna heteroplasmy **was studied** in oocytes and placenta ...

In group 1, the generic *"we"* is used, together with the verb that describes the purpose. That is, the authors assume responsibility for their research. In group 2, *"this paper/study/article"* "does" the describing, rather than the authors themselves. In groups 3 and 4, the textual patterns show commonality in describing what the purpose of the research is or was. Group 5 uses the verb in the infinitive form. This is commonly used in two ways: (i) together with a method component so as to express the idea that the authors adopted a given method to study something or (ii) in structured abstracts[15]. All examples in group 6 use the passive voice. Here, authors put themselves in the background and disguise authorship.

Now let us look at "purposive" verbs. Can you identify them in the examples above? Here are some examples to help you in this task.

1. In this paper we **investigate** the notion ...

---

[15] Structured abstracts are those in which the components are clearly identified. They are most common in health sciences. Here is an example from dentistry: Purpose: To evaluate the time needed to remove ... ; Methods: 40 extracted anterior teeth were mounted in acrylic blocks ... ; Results: Postcement combination significantly affected ...

2. This article **addresses** Internet search problems by considering ...

3. The objective of this study was to **determine** the effects of the ...

4. The purpose here is to **explore** some abstractions that help read ...

5. ... mtdna heteroplasmy was **studied** in oocytes and placenta ...

6.2.2 IDENTIFYING PATTERNS IN YOUR OWN CORPUS

You should now turn to your selected research papers and examine their abstracts. Keep in mind that some abstracts may not include all the typical components. You may find abstracts without explicit description of the purpose of the research. Identify the *purpose* component and answer the questions below:

- What is the preferred pattern for stating the purpose of the research among these papers?
- What "purposive" verbs are used?
- Do any of these verbs appear more often than others?

A question that usually arises in relation to purpose statements is: what verb tense should be used? According to Swales and Feak [39, p. 10], when it comes to the tense of the *purpose* statement in abstracts, the general rule is:

- If a genre-name (e.g., *paper, article, manuscript,* etc.) is used, then the present tense is the preferred tense;
- If the option is for the type of investigation (e.g., *analysis, experiment, tests, survey,* etc.), then the past tense is the preferred choice.

They add that *study* is a special case. It is typically used with the past tense, especially in the health and life sciences, but we also find examples in which *study* occurs with the present tense.

Now examine the verbs in the purpose component of the abstracts from your corpus and answer the following questions:

- How many instances can you find for each of the tenses below:
  - present:
  - past:
  - infinitive:
- Given the abstracts of your corpus, what is the preferred verb tense for the *purpose* component?
- Are there any other tenses that have not been mentioned here?
- Do your findings match Swales and Feak's suggestion?

6.2.3 ABSTRACTS: DESCRIBING RESULTS

Now let us look at ways to describe the findings of your research. We explore textual patterns used in abstracts, as we did before, and then look at verbs commonly employed to describe results. Examine the examples below and:

i   Underline the textual pattern used in each example.
ii   Once all patterns have been identified, pinpoint the "result" verb:

1. In this paper, we demonstrate that current procedures produce ...
2. Our data indicate that this reduction is an early ...
3. These results show that dynamical processes can have ...

4. It is found that interconnects ... are major bottlenecks for ...
5. The paper shows experimentally that when preemption is ...
6. We present results from both simulations and ... which clearly show that our active system is ...
7. Measurements indicate that the system achieves performance comparable to ...
8. The cls is found to vanish when the mean ...
9. Examinations of the experimental results in combination with empirical models suggest that distributions are ...
10. We found no evidence of excess cases corresponding to ...

6.2.4 IDENTIFYING PATTERNS IN ABSTRACTS IN YOUR OWN CORPUS

Once you identify the results component in each selected abstract, try to determine the following:

- What is the preferred pattern in your research field for describing the results?
- What are the typical "result" verbs used in your research field?
- What is the preferred verb tense for the *results* component?

6.3 THE INTRODUCTION SECTION

In the *Introduction* section of a research paper you are expected to provide the reader with a general overview of your research topic. The goal is to demonstrate how your research fits into the field at large. This is usually done by integrating your ideas and arguments with those of others and aligning yourself with a given community, school, or approach [40], [39, p. 117], [41].

In terms of structure, Swales's model for introductions ([5, p. 141], [7, pp. 226–233]) is regarded as fairly prototypical for most, if not all, disciplines. It includes three rhetorical moves:

1. Establishing the territory;
2. Establishing a niche;
3. Occupying the niche.

Thus, a typical introduction usually starts by explaining what is known about the topic and claiming relevance to the field. When reporting previous studies, one can point out weaknesses and gaps so as to indicate what is to come. This may be followed by a description of the novelty of the study and justification of its aims. At the end of the introduction, it is common to present the purpose of the research. You may add your hypotheses, present a brief description of your methods, and highlight significant outcomes. In many research fields, it is standard practice to conclude the introduction section with an outline of the paper.

6.3.1 INTRODUCING WHAT IS KNOWN ABOUT THE TOPIC

When setting the context of your research, you can focus on studies that contribute to that field and demonstrate how your work serves a contribution to a cumulative process [39, p. 117, pp. 141–142]. Here, you are expected to discuss general trends, approaches, patterns and directions, rather than criticizing individual research [39, pp. 141–142].

In this section, we examine textual patterns that are frequently used in introduction sections to present what is known about the topic. Your task is to group them according to these categories:

    i.   the topic has been **extensively** studied;
    ii. the topic has been **moderately** studied;
    iii. the topic has **not** been fully explored and studies are still needed.

You should also underline the textual patterns that support your decision.

1. The significance of ... has been widely acknowledged in the literature.
2. There is considerable debate in the literature about the origins of ...
3. Not only have these issues been gaining considerable currency in various fields ... but they have increasingly been acknowledged within ...
4. A few studies have more directly evaluated the impact of ...
5. There are indications in the literature that the influence of ...
6. There has been less interest in either the organization or practices of ...
7. The new research streams have found increasing attention in the literature and researchers have ...
8. Scholars have repeatedly shown that these factors can have a ...
9. The program is said to have substantially increased ...

6.3.2 DIVERSIFYING PATTERNS

Consider the examples below and answer the questions that follow by consulting COCA.

1. **There is *considerable* debate in the literature about** the origins of ...

   - What other adjectives could be used in the position where *considerable* occurs?

2. **There has been *less* interest in** either the organization or practices of ...

   - let us imagine that your intention is to express the opposite idea, that is, that *there has been* much *interest in* something. In addition to *much*, what other adjectives could be used in the position where *less* occurs?

3. Not only have these issues ... but they **have *increasingly* been *acknowledged*** within the area of ...

   - What adverbs can you use to replace *increasingly* in the sentence above?

   - What verbs can you use to replace *acknowledged*? Make sure you also select the most typical adverbs used with each verb option.

6.3.3 INDICATING GAPS IN THE LITERATURE

It is common in scientific writing to state "gaps" or "weaknesses" in previous work [39, p. 16]. These are related to the currently described research whose purpose is to fill such gap or to provide a contribution toward its solution.

We now examine the textual patterns commonly employed to indicate gaps. Look at the examples below and identify the patterns that reflect such feature.

1. The relationship between ... are not clarified in the more recent studies and remain interesting topics worth exploring.
2. Results from early studies are mixed and little is known about how this affects ...
3. Although the model represents an important advance in the area of ... , two empirical challenges remain.
4. Although such limits are widely viewed as efficient, there is no consensus regarding their efficiency value.
5. A key question remains unanswered: what is the underlying reason behind this decision?

6.3.4 IDENTIFYING PATTERNS IN INTRODUCTIONS IN YOUR OWN CORPUS

Now turn to your set of research papers. Examine the introductory sections and search for other examples of patterns that would also fit in the categories discussed above.

6.3.5 CITING PREVIOUS WORK

Citing the work of others is important in research papers. Citations are usually included in the introductory section of a paper — introductions and review of literature — in order to demonstrate how the current research fits into a wider context.

One important point to bear in mind is that the number of citations and preferred structures used to refer to the work of others can vary from one discipline to another [40], and even from one publication to another within the same discipline. The same can be said about the choice of reporting verbs. These are those verbs whose subject is the cited author(s), such as *found* in the example below.

*Dayrell [9] **found** significant differences between student and published writing in relation to their preferred patterns.*

Here are the most frequent reporting verbs identified by Hyland [40, p. 349] in his analysis of 80 research papers published by leading academic journals from various disciplines.

Philosophy	say, suggest, argue, claim, point out, propose, think
Sociology	argue, suggest, describe, note, analyze, discuss
Applied Linguistics	suggest, argue, show, explain, find, point out
Marketing	suggest, argue, demonstrate, propose, show
Biology	describe, find, report, show, suggest, observe
Electronic Eng.	propose, use, describe, show, publish
Mechanical Eng.	describe, show, report, discuss
Physics	develop, report, study

In their analysis of student academic writing, Thompson and Tribble [41] demonstrated that novice writers tend to be fairly repetitive in terms of the constructions used to cite previous work as well as the reporting verbs used in citations.

This section focuses on reporting verbs in citations. Examine the examples below and answer the following questions:

i What is the reporting verb in each example?

ii What is the tense of the reporting verb? The options are: simple present (e.g., *shows*), simple past (*showed*), and present perfect (*has/have shown*).

1. Marriott et al. (2012) reported that the most current estimates of ...
2. Steven (2003) combined data on domestic and international reserves ...
3. A large number of previous studies have examined how such differences can interfere ...
4. Lee (2012) provides a comprehensive review of the literature on approaches for determining ...
5. Graham (2008) found that international reserves are more difficult ...
6. Thompson and Walters (2010) argue that the approach should be adopted ...

You should now examine the introductory sections of the research papers in your study corpus and answer the following questions:

i   What are the five most frequent reporting verbs in your research field?

ii What is the prevailing verb tense when citing previous studies?

6.3.6 DESCRIBING THE STRUCTURE OF THE PAPER

Last, but not least, let us now look at the last paragraph of introductions. As mentioned earlier, for many research fields, it is standard practice to conclude with an outline of the structure of the paper.

This paragraph is usually structured within a limited range of options, which in fact makes it relatively easy to write. Below are two examples of how to present the structure of your paper. Consider the following structure of a paper and fill in the blanks in the paragraphs that follow.

Section 1: Introduction
Section 2: Review of key methodological debates on segregation
Section 3: Description of our experimental design and simulation procedures
Section 4: Results
Section 5: Discussion
Section 6: Overview of the key findings and directions for future research.

- The remainder of the paper is organized as follows. We first _____ . This is followed by___. The results of the experiments____in Section 4 and ____in Section 5. The paper___.
- This paper begins by ___. Second, ___. Section 4 _____ and is followed by ___ on the impact of _____. The last section _____.

6.3.7 IDENTIFYING PATTERNS IN METHODS SECTIONS

In academic writing, differences among disciplines are mostly seen in the methods and results sections [7, p. 219]. For example, not all research fields call for a separate section to describe methods. If that is the case, the methods are often described elsewhere in the paper. For example, some disciplines prefer to include methodology in the introductory sections.

If there is a methods section, it usually includes the data or material used in the research, procedures, and, in some cases, equipment, tools, software, and statistical analyses [7, p. 219]. Here, we are expected to provide evidence that we have carefully considered the conditions for testing hypotheses or answering research questions.

This section explores the structure and useful constructions to describe methodological procedures. Examine the papers in **your** study corpus, and answer the following questions:

i.   Is there a *methods* section?

ii. If not, are methods described elsewhere?

Now let us consider papers with a *methods* section. The extent of details in *methods* sections can vary from one research field to another. Swales [7, pp. 220–223] proposes a continuum for representing how *methods* sections are usually written. At one end, we have clipped methods sections. These are condensed and brief, and common for research fields whose methods are already well established. Thus, there is no need to provide background information nor to justify choices. Acronyms and citations are frequent since authors may simply refer the reader elsewhere rather than describing the method themselves. In general, subsections and definitions are not required. At the other end of the continuum, we have elaborated *methods* sections. Here, authors need to offer details of the procedures and justify their decisions. Definitions and citations are usually needed. Elaborated *methods* sections tend to be long and may be divided into subsections.

Consider the papers in your study corpus and answer:

1. How detailed are the *methods* sections in your research field?

Here is Swales's categorization ([7, p. 223]) within the proposed continuum for typical methods sections of some research fields:

Clipped		Elaborated
Sociolinguistics		Education
Physics	Language Sciences	Psychology
Chemistry	Public Health	Phonetics
Biology	Earth Sciences	Cognitive Linguistics
Medicine		Sociology

In relation to other sections of a research paper, methods sections are usually thought to be relatively easy to write, but not always exciting to read. Let us look at two constructions that are not often used by non-native novice writers and could be useful for enlivening your methods section. These are: *how* sentences and left dislocation. They are fairly common in *methods* sections, but can be used in any section of a paper.

HOW SENTENCES: BY + ING

How sentences are useful for explaining how something has been done. They include the preposition *by* followed by a verb in the gerund form (e.g., *by using*). Here is an example:

Differences between the distributions were assessed **by applying** a statistical test significance.

Can you rewrite the sentences below using *by* + *ing* ?

1. We applied the Kappa statistic test to determine the level of agreement among analysts.
   We determined _____ .

2. One way to control the cost and schedule of a project is to keep the same techniques and methods across all phases.
   We controlled _____.

LEFT-DISLOCATION

Left dislocations occur when you place some material on the left of the grammatical subject [39, p. 207]. This is the case of the clause in **bold**, which is placed before the subject " *we.*"

To avoid such difficulties we applied a novel method, which will be described in detail in the next section.

Left dislocation is common in *methods* sections to justify one's decision or choice. It has two important effects [39, p. 224]: (i) to anticipate doubts arising in the reader's mind about a procedure, and (ii) to suggest that the author has worked out the reasons for adopting a given procedure, irrespective of whether that is actually the case.

Now let us look at the examples below. Can you left-dislocate them?

1. These approaches seem to be highly effective once they have been established.
2. All patients had negative test results for the hepatitis B surface antigen before starting therapy.
3. We have collected a validation sample and used precise measurements of numerous independent variables in order to assess misclassification.

DIVERSIFYING VERBS: THE CASE OF USE

The verb "use" appears very frequently in academic writing, and in methods sections in particular. However, novice writers tend to overuse it, perhaps because they are not aware of other options that would also fit in the context.

Consult COCA and identify other verbs that could replace "use" in the sentences below:

1. Different methods are **used** to measure the level of oxygen in the blood.
2. This approach was **used** because different parameter sets can perform with different levels of success under the criteria **used**.

6.3.8 IDENTIFYING PATTERNS IN RESULTS AND DISCUSSION SECTIONS

In *results* and *discussion* sections, we aim to demonstrate and discuss how our work contributes to the research field and emphasize the value of our research. Thus, "*rather than stepping back to allow results to neutrally speak for themselves*" [42, p. 72], the idea is to lead the reader through the results of interest and explain why they are of interest. Some research fields have these as two separate sections; that is, you describe your findings in the *results* section and then provide your interpretation and evaluation in the *discussion* section. Other research fields opt for providing all the information in one single section, thus interpreting the findings while describing them.

Irrespective of whether you choose to have two separate sections or a single one, it is typical to follow three basic rhetorical moves when describing and interpreting the findings of your research [43, 44]:

1. Setting the scene
2. Presenting the findings
3. Discussing findings

In most cases, this is done, in fact, through a sequence of repeated cycles rather than by presenting the overall development in just one go [45, p. 203], [44].

Before you present your findings, you are expected to explain how observations were converted to analyzable data and to provide evidence that the conditions for testing the hypotheses or answering the research questions have been successfully met [43]. We usually do this in the *methods* section, but you may sometimes revisit some of the most relevant points in your *results* section.

PRESENTING YOUR FINDINGS

Here are some of the questions to bear in mind when describing findings:

- What comes first: general or specific results?
- How are you going to handle negative results, that is, those that refute your hypothesis/assumption?
- Should you mention the data that has been discarded from the analysis?

Another important decision involves determining which data you should convert into tables, figures, and/or graphs. The basic rule is to use these devices to summarize your major findings. Before displaying a table, figure, and/or graph, it is always advisable to introduce it to your reader by explaining what data it contains. Here is an example:

In Table I we show the percentage of subjects in each experimental condition.

You will often find the textual pattern "Table *n* shows (the)," where "Table" could be replaced by "Figure" or "Graph" and *n* indicates the number of the entity within the document. However, since neither tables nor figures have the ability to show, a more elegant pattern would be "In Table/Figure/Graph we show ..." Consult COCA and answer: What other verbs can we use here instead of " *shows* "?

- Table *n* shows (the):
- Figure *n* shows (the):
- Graph *n* shows (the):

Once you have presented a table, figure, and/or graph, you can then refer back to it and point out the results of interest. Here is one way of doing it:

As shown in Graph 1, *unemployment rate declined by 2.4 percent in the year 2011.*

Consult COCA and identify which other verbs we can use instead of *shown* within the pattern *as shown in Table.*

Earlier in this chapter, we discussed a number of patterns that are commonly used to describe findings, such as *in this paper we demonstrate that, our data indicate that, these results show that, it is found that, we found that.* We now focus on constructions to discuss our results.

DISCUSSING FINDINGS

Discussion is said to be the most difficult section for novice researchers to write. This is probably because personal involvement is expected, and writers have to put themselves in the foreground to present their arguments and evaluative comments [42, p. 73]. The focus is on the research described in the paper and "*the work of others ... are introduced for confirmation, comparison, or contradistinction*" [7, p. 235].

Examine the patterns below and identify which corresponds with each of the ten sample phrases that follow:

- presenting findings,

- explaining findings,
- the author's interpretation of the results,
- expressing comparing the result with existing literature,
- expressing the author's opinion.

1. Our data indicate that
2. In line with previous studies
3. It is crucial that
4. It could be argued that
5. The results from our models provide evidence consistent with previous work on
6. This may be due to the fact that
7. Our findings are highly relevant for
8. We found that
9. One possible reason for these differences is that
10. ... thus implying that

In the concluding section of research papers, in addition to revisiting the main findings of the study, you may also [7, pp. 235–238]:

- Stress its main contributions and implications;
- State its limitations;
- Make suggestions for future studies.

Examine the concluding sections of the papers from your own corpus and answer:

i   Are the rhetorical moves above found in your sample papers?
ii Can you identify the textual patterns commonly used in them?

6.3.10 IDENTIFYING PATTERNS IN ACKNOWLEDGMENTS

We conclude this chapter by looking at acknowledgments. As Swales and Feak [45, p. 204] explain, "they provide an opportunity for you to show that you are a member of a community and have benefited from that membership." Here is a list of topics that you may include in your *acknowledgments* section: financial support, thanks, disclaimers, reference to previous versions of the paper, mentioning that the paper was based on other work — for example, a thesis (ibid.).

Examine the acknowledgments in your set of research papers, and look for patterns that you could use in your own writing.

6.4 WHAT HAVE WE LEARNED?

In this chapter we have learned about textual patterns that are found in research papers. We first introduced the concept of patterns and explained the significant role they play in scientific writing. Then, we showed how these patterns can be identified and used by examining key aspects of the common sections in a standard research paper.

CHAPTER 7

Osvaldo N. Oliveira Jr.
Ethel Schuster
Haim Levkowitz

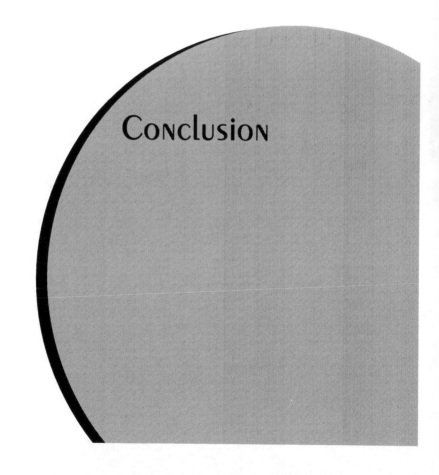

CONCLUSION

Our main aim in this book has been to provide the readers, particularly graduate students, with a guide to assist them in the writing of effective papers. We attempted to do this in two ways: first, by describing a corpus-based strategy that is especially useful for non-native speakers of English in order to minimize the influence of their mother tongue, and second, by presenting a set of software tools that may assist students in producing and assessing the outline of their papers. Within the corpus-based approach, one may implement learning-by-example strategies, which have several advantages. In addition to allowing the student to express him or herself using proper scientific language, these strategies serve the purpose of familiarizing the student with scientific discourse. This strategy has been tested over many years in scientific writing courses at the University of São Paulo, Brazil. It has proven successful, but requires that the student invest considerable time and effort in building his or her corpus and practicing writing exercises.

The time-consuming nature of the learning process in scientific writing motivated us to develop software-writing tools, some of which are described in this book. These tools tend to be underused, often because their availability is limited or because they are tailored to specific areas, but most significantly be- cause few students are aware of their existence. We hope that this book brings greater awareness about the tools that are available. We believe that recent and ongoing technological advances in the field of natural language processing will continue to encourage researchers and developers around the world to create more generic, user-friendly tools. We hope that our step-by-step guide to using the tools described will give readers a better understanding of these tools and their usefulness.

Besides the utilitarian perspective of this book as a guide, we believe that readers can benefit greatly from learning the fundamentals of scientific writing and corpus linguistics, as the field of scientific writing is now well established and is based on underlying principles at the core of the scientific method. Learning to write effectively also necessitates proper use of the scientific method. For this reason, several chapters in this book are devoted to describing its principles. Studying the structure of a scientific paper from a more formal perspective and dissecting generic models may, in fact, aid in making writing practices more effective. By the same token, we feel that teaching the learn-by-example strategies would not be complete without an explanation of the fundamentals of corpus linguistics. Though the intention of the book is not to teach English, non-native speakers will realize the value of acquiring knowledge on language use from a corpus.

As scientists working in a variety of fields, we were able to evaluate and confirm the value and impact of learning the principles of corpus linguistics and scientific writing on our research and careers. This was our main motivation for putting together a book that covers both the theoretical and practical aspects of scientific writing.

Interested readers can find further information, and inspiration, in various books dedicated to scientific writing (see for instance [46-52]), perhaps starting with the oldest and still one of the most influential "Elements of Style", by Strunk and White [46].

Appendix A

Components and Strategies for each section of a scientific paper

Here we show the characterization of each section of a scientific paper into components (C) and strategies (S).

A.1 Abstract: Components and strategies

C1: Setting
S1 Argue about the topic's prominence
S2 Familiarize terms, objects, or processes
S3 Cite previous research results
S4 Introduce hypotheses
C2: Types of Gap
S1 Cite problems/difficulties
S2 Cite needs/requirements
S3 Cite missing issues in previous research
C3: Purpose
S1 Indicate main purpose
S2 Specify the purpose
S3 Introduce additional purposes
S4 Introduce purpose with methods
S5 Introduce purpose with results
C4: Methods and Materials
S1 List criteria or conditions
S2 Describe methods and materials
S3 Justify chosen methods and materials
C5: Main Results
S1 Describe the results
S2 Outline the results
S3 Comments about the results

C6: Conclusion

S1 Outline conclusions

S2 Outline contributions/importance of research

S3 Outline suggestions

S4 List issues/topics addressed in the research

A.2 INTRODUCTION: COMPONENTS AND STRATEGIES

C1: Setting

S1 Introduce the research topic within the research area

S2 Familiarize terms, objects, or processes

S3 Argue about the topic's prominence

C2: Review

S1 Historical review

S2 Current trends

S3 General-to-specific ordering of citations

S4 Progress in the area

S5 Requirements for moving forward in the area

S6 State-of-the-art

S7 Compound reviews of the literature and their gaps

S8 Citations grouped by approaches

S9 Citing authors' previous study

S10 Reviewing relevant results

C3: Types of Gap

S1 Unresolved conflict or problem among previous studies

S2 Limitations of previous work

S3 Raise questions

C4: Purpose

S1 Indicate main purpose

S1A Solve conflict among authors

S1B Present a novel approach, method, or technique

S1C Present an improvement in a research topic

S1D Present an extension of authors' prior work

S1E Propose an alternative approach

S1F Present comparative research work
S2 Specify the purpose
S3 Introduce additional purposes
S4 Present the purpose with results
C5: Methods and Materials
S1 List criteria or conditions
S2 Describe methods and materials
S3 Justify chosen methods and materials
C6: Main Results
S1 Present/emphasize results
S2 Comments about the results
C7: Value of the Research
S1 State importance of the research
C8: Layout of the article
S1A Outline the parts of the paper

A.3 METHODS AND MATERIALS: COMPONENTS AND STRATEGIES

C1: Methods and Materials
S1 List materials used in the research
S2 Describe source of materials used
S3 Detail information about materials
C2: Methods and Procedures
S1 Document experimental methods used
S2 Detail procedures used to properly carry out the methods
S3 Justify the procedures employed
C3: Equipment
S1 Describe equipment used
S2 Analyze data
S3 Explain procedures used to analyze data
C4: Data Analysis
S1 Data analysis procedure
C5: Main Results
S1 Describe the results

A.4 Results: Components and Strategies

C1: Setting
S1 Familiarize terms, objects, or methods
C2: Bibliography/Reference
S1 Discuss authors' previous research
S2 Discuss other authors' previous research
S3 Compare current with authors' previous research
S4 Compare research with other authors' research
C3: Purpose
S1 Cite purpose
C4: Methods and Materials
S1 Cite methods
C5: Main Results
S1 Emphasize results
S2 Place results in context
S3 Present results
S4 Discuss results
S5 Justify results
S6 Speculate on the results
S7 Present an explanation

A.5 Discussion: Components and Strategies

C1: Revisit Setting
S1 Argue about the topic's prominence within research area
S2 Familiarize terms, objects, or methods
C2: Literature Review
S1 Summary of research
S2 Describe authors' previous research
S3 Compare current with authors' previous research
S4 Compare research with other authors' research
S5 Review literature
C3: Review Purpose
S1 Revisit purpose or initial hypothesis

C4: Review Main Results
S1 Describe most important finding
S2 Describe speculations or deductions
S3 Describe results
S4 Discuss results
S5 Discuss unexpected results
C5: Review Methods
S1 Discuss methods
C6: Present Conclusions
S1 Discuss research limitations
S2 Discuss research implications
S3 Discuss suggestions
S4 Discuss future research
S5 Mention funding agencies
S6 Thank collaborators/participants

A.6 Conclusions: Components and strategies

C1: Setting
S1 Familiarize terms, objects, or processes
C2: Purpose
S1 Indicate main purpose
C3: Methods and Materials
S1 Describe methods and materials
C4: Main Results
S1 Describe results
S2 Explain/speculate about results
C5: Conclusion
S1 Outline research limitations
S2 Outline research implications
S3 Outline suggestions
S4 Cite authors' previous research
S5 Cite previous research
S6 Discuss research contributions/importance

BIBLIOGRAPHY

[1] S.G. Trost, D.S. Ward, S.M. Moorehead, P.D. Watson, W. Riner, and J.R. Burke. Validity of the computer science and applications (csa) activity monitor in children. *Medicine and science in sports and exercise*, 30(4):629–633, 1998.

[2] C. Ecker, J. Suckling, S.C. Deoni, M.V. Lombardo, E.T. Bullmore, S. Baron-Cohen, M. Catani, P. Jezzard, A. Barnes, A.J. Bailey, et al. Brain anatomy and its relationship to behavior in adults with autism spectrum disorder: a multicenter magnetic resonance imaging study. *Archives of General Psychiatry*, 69(2):195–209, 2012.

[3] M. Ristich. Rhetorical analysis in three easy steps. *WSU Teaching: The Wayne State Writing Teacher's Forum*, October 2011.

[4] C.C. Walsh. Write for computer: Author guidelines. *IEEE Computer*, 2014.

[5] J. Swales. *Genre analysis: English in academic and research settings*. Cambridge University Press, 1990.

[6] J. Swales. *Aspects of article introductions*. Language Studies Unit, University of Aston in Birmingham, 1981.

[7] J. Swales. *Research genres: Explorations and applications*. Ernst Klett Sprachen, 2004.

[8] G. Parodi. The rhetorical organization of the textbook genre across disciplines: A "colony-in-loops"? *Discourse Studies*, 12(2):195–222, 2010.

[9] A. Stevenson. *Oxford Dictionary of English*. Oxford reference online premium. OUP Oxford, 2010.

[10] E. Pitler. Attacking parsing bottlenecks with unlabeled data and relevant factorizations. In *Proceedings of the 50th Annual Meeting of the Association for Computational Linguistics: Long Papers - Volume 1*, ACL '12, pages 768–776, Stroudsburg, PA, USA, 2012.

[11] K.C. Fraser, J.A. Meltzer, N.L. Graham, C. Leonard, G. Hirst, S.E. Black, and E. Rochon. Automated classification of primary progressive aphasia subtypes from narrative speech transcripts. *Cortex*, 2012.

[12] R. Weissberg and S. Buker. *Writing up research*. Prentice Hall Englewood Cliffs, NJ, 1990.

[13] S.M. Aluísio and O.N. Oliveira, Jr. . A detailed schematic structure of research papers introductions: An application in support-writing tools. *Revista de La Sociedad Espanyola Para El Procesamiento Del Lenguage Natural*, 19:141–147, 1996.

[14] A.C. Weaver and B.B. Morrison. Social networking. *Computer*, 41(2):97–100, 2008.

[15] J.M.A. Carnall, C.A. Waudby, A.M. Belenguer, M.C.A. Stuart, J.J-P Peyralans, and S. Otto. Mechanosensitive self-replication driven by self-organization. *Science*, 327(5972):1502–1506, 2010.

[16] J. Eid, A. Fehr, J. Gray, K. Luong, J. Lyle, G. Otto, P. Peluso, D. Rank, P. Baybayan, B. Bettman, et al. Real-time DNA sequencing from single polymerase molecules. *Science*, 323(5910):133–138, 2009.

[17] P. Diplas, C.L. Dancey, A.O. Celik, M. Valyrakis, K. Greer, and T. Akar. The role of impulse on the initiation of particle movement under turbulent flow conditions. *Science*, 322(5902):717–720, 2008.

[18] T. Yeung, G.E. Gilbert, J. Shi, J. Silvius, A. Kapus, and S. Grinstein. Membrane phosphatidylserine regulates surface charge and protein localization. *Science*, 319(5860):210–213, 2008.

[19] D.J. Bornhop, J.C. Latham, A. Kussrow, D.A. Markov, R.D. Jones, and H.S. Sørensen. Free-solution, label-free molecular interactions studied by back-scattering interferometry. *Science*, 317(5845):1732–1736, 2007.

[20] L. Schröder, T.J. Lowery, C. Hilty, D.E. Wemmer, and A. Pines. Molecular imaging using a targeted magnetic resonance hyperpolarized biosensor. *Science*, 314(5798):446–449, 2006.

[21] H.D. Rowland, W.P. King, J.B. Pethica, and G.L.W. Cross. Molecular confinement accelerates deformation of entangled polymers during squeeze flow. *Science*, 322(5902):720–724, 2008.

[22] J.R. Genoves, V.D. Feltrim, C. Dayrell, and S.M. Aluísio. Automatically detecting schematic structure components of english abstracts: building a high accuracy classifier for the task. In *International Workshop on Natural Language Processing for Educational Resources in conjunction with the International Conference RANLP 2007*, pages 23–29, 2007.

[23] C. Dayrell, A. Candido Jr, G. Lima, D. Machado Jr, A.A. Copestake, V.D. Feltrim, S.E.O. Tagnin, and S.M. Aluísio. Rhetorical move detection in English abstracts: Multi-label sentence classifiers and their annotated corpora. In *LREC*, pages 1604–1609, 2012.

[24] S. Teufel and M. Moens. Summarizing scientific articles: experiments with relevance and rhetorical status. *Computational Linguistics*, 28(4):409–445, 2002.

[25] V.D. Feltrim, J.M. Pelizzoni, S. Teufel, M.G.V. Nunes, and S.M. Aluísio. Applying argumentative zoning in an automatic critiquer of academic writing. In *Advances in Artificial Intelligence—SBIA 2004*, pages 214–223. Springer, 2004.

[26] S.M. Aluísio, E. Schuster, V.D. Feltrim, A. Pessoa, and O.N. Oliveira Jr. Evaluating scientific abstracts with a genre-specific rubric. In *AIED*, pages 738–740, 2005.

[27] L. Anthony. *Concordancing with AntConc: An Introduction to Tools and Techniques in Corpus Linguistics (Summary of JACET 2006 workshop).* JACET Newsletter, Issue 55, 2006.

[28] M. Scott. *WordSmith Tools Manual, Version 6.* Lexical Analysis Software Ltd, Liverpool, 2011.

[29] T. Kinnunen, H. Leisma, M. Machunik, T. Kakkonen, and J-L. Lebrun. Swan-scientific writing assistant: a tool for helping scholars to write reader-friendly manuscripts. In *Proceedings of the Demonstrations at the 13th Conference of the European Chapter of the Association for Computational Linguistics,* pages 20–24. Association for Computational Linguistics, 2012.

[30] D.R. Amancio, S.M. Aluísio, O.N. Oliveira Jr., and L.F. Costa. Complex networks analysis of language complexity. *EPL (Europhysics Letters),* 100(5):58002, 2012.

[31] K. Hyland. Academic clusters: Text patterning in published and postgraduate writing. *International Journal of Applied Linguistics,* 18(1):41–62, 2008.

[32] K. Hyland. As can be seen: Lexical bundles and disciplinary variation. *English for specific purposes,* 27(1):4–21, 2008.

[33] J.R. Nattinger, J.S DeCarrico, and J.R. Nattinger. *Lexical phrases and language teaching,* volume 1. Oxford University Press Oxford, 1992.

[34] R.H. Haswell. *Gaining ground in college writing: Tales of development and interpretation.* Southern Methodist University Press, 1991.

[35] J.C.P. Milton and K. Hyland. Assertions in students' academic essays: A comparison of English ns and nns student writers. *Language,* 1996.

[36] C. Dayrell. Frequency and lexico-grammatical patterns of sense-related verbs in English and Portuguese abstracts. In R. Xiao, editor, *Proceedings of the International Symposium on Using Corpora in Contrastive and Translation Studies,* pages 486–507, Newcastle, 2010. Cambridge Scholars Publishing.

[37] C. Dayrell. *Corpora and academic English teaching: lexico-grammatical patterns in abstracts written by Brazilian graduate students.* 2011.

[38] K. Hyland. *Disciplinary discourses: Social interactions in academic writing.* University of Michigan Press, 2004.

[39] J.M. Swales and C.B. Feak. *Abstracts and the Writing of Abstracts.* Michigan: University of Michigan Press, 2009.

[40] K. Hyland. Academic attribution: Citation and the construction of disciplinary knowledge. *Applied Linguistics,* 20(3):341–367, 1999.

[41] P. Thompson and C. Tribble. Looking at citations: Using corpora in English for academic purposes. *Language Learning and Technology*, 5(3):91–105, 2001.

[42] K. Hyland. *Academic discourse: English in a global context.* Bloomsbury Publishing, 2009.

[43] D.J. Bem. *Writing the Empirical Journal Article.* The Compleat Academic: A Career Guide, Washington, DC, 2002.

[44] R. Yang and A. Desmond. Research articles in applied linguistics: moving from results to conclusions. *English for Specific Purposes*, 22(4):365 – 385, 2003.

[45] J.M. Swales and C.B. Feak. *Academic writing for graduate students: Essential Tasks and Skills: A Course for Nonnative Speakers of English (English for Specific Purposes)*, volume 1. University of Michigan Press Ann Arbor, MI, 1994.

[46] W. Strunk and E.B. White. *The Elements of Style*, (4th ed.). Longman, 1999.

[47] R.A. Day. *How to Write & Publish a Scientific Paper*, (5th ed.). Oryx Press, 1998.

[48] M. Alley. *The Craft of Scientific Writing*, (3rd ed.). Springer, 1996.

[49] M. Zeiger. *Essentials of Writing Biomedical Research Papers*, (2nd ed.). McGraw-Hill Professional, 1999.

[50] J.K. Peat, E. Elliott, L. Baur and V. Keena. *Scientific Writing: Easy When You Know How.* BMJ Books, 2002.

[51] J. R. Matthews and R.W. Matthews. *Successful Scientific Writing: A Step-by-step Guide for the Biological and Medical Sciences*, (3rd ed.). Cambridge University Press, 2007.

[52] H. Glasman-Deal. *Science Research Writing for Non-native Speakers of English.* Imperial College Press, 2009.

Made in the USA
Lexington, KY
07 November 2015